BACK UP NORTH

THE CHEBOYGAN DAILY TRIBUNE COLUMNS

BY

DONALD HOLMES LEWIS

BACK UP NORTH

The Cheboygan Daily Tribune Columns

Straits Area Publishing
P.O. Box 11 • 231-627-5647
Cheboygan, MI 49721
www.straitsareapublishing.com

Front cover drawing by David Savic.

ACKNOWLEDGEMENTS

The first year *Back Up North* columns were written from the spring of 2009 until the early summer of 2010 and published by the *Cheboygan Daily Tribune* during that period. Fifty columns appear in this book. There are so many people I need to thank for helping both write and publish the columns that I apologize in advance to those I might forget to mention.

First of all, I'd like to express my appreciation to Sally, my wife of nearly 30 years who both reluctantly and encouragingly put up with my incessant use of her as the principal foil for telling the stories. Sally's the real writer in our family. She writes under the name Sally Savic (you can Google her or search for her books and stories at Amazon.com). She critiqued my style, helped me formulate the voice I knew was inside me, and ignored me in self defense when she had to.

Second, there's no way I could have written *Back Up North* without the help of Mike Eads, until just recently the Editor of the *Cheboygan Daily Tribune*. Mike recognized something in my first submission, a point of view worth printing. He chopped and cut and helped me rewrite nearly every story. And thanks to Gary Lamberg, Publisher at the paper. Gary supported the whole concept of writing about moving to the Straits Area and making the transition to full time resident. He did the same a year before Sally and I arrived.

I've taken tons of liberties and a basket full of poetic license in including real people from the Cheboygan area in the stories. Those mentioned have been more than gracious about it. Thanks to everyone for not deciding I needed a good tar and feathering.

Most important, I'd like to express my profound appreciation to the readers of the Tribune who followed my columns week in and week out. There were flurries of email from time to time. Sometimes folks would stop me in the grocery or on the street and tell me how much they liked the most recent story. Every moment like that energized and inspired me in ways I can't describe.

Lastly, huge thanks to Scott Beard at Straits Area Publishing. It takes a pontoon full of work to get an imperfect manuscript ready for the real world and that's what Scott and his staff have done.

Donald Holmes Lewis
August, 2010

FOREWARD

Don and Sally Lewis arrived at their cottage near Cheboygan, suddenly new year-round residents of Northern Michigan. Like so many transplants, there was a significant adjustment from life in the city. Dreaming of retirement on the lake is often much different than the reality one faces after making the move.

Somewhere during the transition Don decided to write about settling in to their new life on the shoreline. Somehow he convinced the editor of the *Cheboygan Daily Tribune* that our readers would be interested in hearing about that first year on the lake.

Turns out he was right.

Don began the *Back Up North* column that ran weekly in the paper and it developed a following. Apparently, quite a few folks had a similar experience adjusting to small town life and living full time in vacationland.

After a year of columns, Don has compiled *Back Up North* into a book. Readers can sit down and get the full story of the transition to full time residency on Mullett Lake between two covers, rather than waiting for a new chapter every Friday in the Tribune.

Don Lewis writes from the heart. He describes the emotional rollercoaster of a life uprooted and replanted in a very different place.

Readers get the sense of a transplant, struggling to grow. Eventually, the roots begin to take hold, uncertainty is replaced by engagement. The transplant begins to thrive, nurtured by new friends and fertilized by new ground.

Congratulations on your new book, Don.

Gary Lamberg, Publisher
Cheboygan Daily Tribune

Table of Contents

May 2009 - June 2010

The Hotel Topinabee
Monday, May 4th, 2009

Sometimes the urge for a great sandwich hits me like a kick from a mule and I have to respond, so I stopped at The Breakers in Topinabee for an olive burger.

Maybe it was the hint of summer along Mullett Lake as I drove south on the Straits Highway. There were docks going out with urgency. A few fishermen drifted out on the still blue water. Pickup trucks with empty boat trailers were parked near the public access.

Whatever it was, it made me hungry.

Sitting at the bar waiting to gorge myself, I asked my fellow patrons about what Topinabee was like back when steam and then diesel engines pulled passengers cars along the shore, stopping at the station in town.

Introducing herself with a smile, longtime resident Dolores Palmer offered images from the early 1950s: the old hotel with its elegant bar, the golf course above it to the west, and old Fords lining both sides of Old 27. People used to pour into Topinabee in the warmer months when the train made its scheduled early evening stop; salesmen, sturgeon and perch aficionados, and summer folk eager for a week's vacation by the lake.

Dolores referred me to the old train station turned library, and I thanked her as I wiped the mayonnaise from the corners of my mouth. I've always had an obsession for the ghosts of earlier days in the places I travel. Now that I'm making a permanent home on the west shore of Mullett Lake, my quirky need to see into the past required some serious attention.

At the library, Patty and Elizabeth welcomed me to the not-so-distant era of Topinabee as Michigan Central Railroad's premier resort stop along Mullett Lake. Old photographs of the village in four gigantic black binders were placed before me on a long table.

I began with the written histories. The name Topinabee comes from an old Native American, Chief Topinabee, who lived in Grayling. Henry H. Pike was a good friend of the chief and he was about to open Pike's Summer Tavern and Casino in 1882 in the location known as Portage, and he needed a good name ("Big Bear's Heart" in Odawa).

I was fascinated right away by the pictures and stories about the old artesian wells of Topinabee. The bottled water from the Sanitas Springs along the track by the hotel was world famous, and the MCRR picked up loads of it every time they stopped. The articles said the wells had been buried many years ago under blacktop and stone, and local residents disagreed about where they were.

It was the photos of old Hotel Top-in-a-bee erected after Pike's place burnt down, however, that garnered most of my curiosity; images of people in straw hats and bloomers picnicking, playing golf at the long lost Topinabee Golf and Country Club, and welcoming the motor launches Romeo and Juliet to the great pier jutting into the lake.

I eventually said my goodbyes to the library staff and started walking along what used to be the track line a hundred yards north to the site of the hotel, now an empty lot between two beautiful summer cottages. As I stood gazing out onto the water, a cold spring breeze picked up off the lake. I thought about the people in the photographs, a girl running down the pier from a newly arrived launch, the waitress staff proudly standing on the outside stairway, a handsome chef eagerly awaiting his guests in an empty dining room filled with white linens and chandeliers.

They all seemed happy to be getting the magical season started again, and wanted me to lead the way.

The Other Side of the Lake
Friday, May 29th, 2009

On Memorial Day, I decided to drive all the way around Mullett Lake. It was a brilliant late spring morning and the wind was a steady thirty miles an hour from the east. White caps rolled over my dock like ocean waves. I had never truly investigated the lands on the opposite side of the blue water though I'd thought of doing it for years. Always too busy. Always an excuse. Now that we were residents of Cheboygan County, not knowing much about the area across our blue water was bothering me the way a crying baby does when you're concentrating on writing. This day I had nothing planned; all the yard chores were done and only if I made up a new repair job out of thin air would I have another reason to deny my natural curiosity about the other shore. There were no story deadlines looming.

I started north from our cottage in my old Jeep Cherokee along the Straits Highway and turned right on Route 33. Crossing over the Cheboygan River, I checked out the quiet flowing waters hoping to see the pontoon and speedboat flotillas of summer, but cold clear weather had kept the boats mostly on their hoists for the holiday weekend. It made me sad for all the proprietors who count on river traffic to make a living.

Since I'd been to the Hack-ma-Tack restaurant many times, I skipped the first turnoff and continued to the Other Road. I followed the straight line gravel south along the northern most bay of Mullett and turned southeast along McDonald Road. Beautiful cottages. Watercraft everywhere eager to set sail. Green yards and pines and birch.

Then the scenery changed and so did my plans for the day.

Forced by dead end streets and "no outlet" signs back towards the highway, I climbed the half mile long eastern slope towards the top of the hill. Beautiful farms with fresh grasses in their fields stretched out on either side of the road. This was high ground. I parked over a culvert and reached for my binoculars. Leaning out the window, I trained the lenses on my shoreline across the way. The view was spectacular. I could see Dodge Point clearly. I could make out the colors of the cars and pickups racing along the western side.

After turning south again on 33, I ran into two stranded Harley riders at the intersection leading to Aloha Beach. The sun was rolling across the sky to early afternoon, the wind still howled, and I saw from a distance their exasperation with one of the motorcycles. I touched the brakes on the Jeep and pulled over.

It was a couple in their early forties. Good looking, handsome even. Sandy beginning-to-turn-grey long hair. Black boots, leather leggings and jackets. Scarves tight to their necks as protection from the frosty air. Helmets on the back racks. They were both staring at the carburetor of the woman's bike.

"Can I help you guys?" I said walking the shoulder.

"I don't know how," said the man. We introduced ourselves. He told me they were from Ann Arbor and on their way to Mackinaw City. He said he'd called the number on his Harley-Davidson Roadside Service Plan card but couldn't get anyone on the line. "They'll call me back in a minute or so. You ride?"

"Oh no, sorry," I said. "I like four wheels under me."

"You mean you've never been on a Harley?

"That's right."

He took his helmet from the back of his bike, removed his leather jacket, and handed them to me, explaining that Sheila would be happy to initiate me, that he'd stay and watch the dead machine and wait for the call. He said it was a great ride back south to 68, a straight shot.

As I settled into my seat behind Sheila, he pointed to the mature apple trees in the front yard of the farm beside us.

"Look at those trees. This area must have produced a lot of fruit sixty or seventy years ago. My family was in the business down south for three generations. Until my dad passed away."

He smiled. Sheila kicked down on the starter and the next thing I knew we were flying down the highway, my arms tightly around her waist. Driving the shoreline would have to wait for another day.

Carpenter Ants in the Back Cabin
Friday, July 10th, 2009

This past Tuesday I made another list. I had a lot of things on it I wanted to do, almost fifteen total, and a couple Sally put on it for me. My stuff started with "Split More Wood" but her two stared at me in a way that blurred everything else: "Ants" and "Mice."

After coffee, she led me across the yard, up the outside stairway, and into to the back cabin bedroom over the garage. In the smallest bedroom, the one you can hardly fit a single bed into, she pointed to the wall where she'd pulled back a piece of duct tape that someone, me, had placed over a hole in the wall five years ago.

"Carpenter ants. Look at the saw dust. I can almost hear them chewing on our wood for breakfast."

"I'll call the pest control people."

"You are the pest control people."

"What about the mice?"

"They're not eating the house."

At the Do It Center store, a man with a red vest walked me down the aisle where you select weapons for this kind of war. Winking at me from their places on the shelves were the WMD of insect killers. There was one, the Hot Shot Fogger, which drew me to the label.

"What's in this stuff?" I asked innocently.

"Bug killer for the most part."

When the man left me alone, I went through an amateur analysis of ingredients on all the different products. I had to use my reading glasses the print was so small. All I could discern was the simple fact that whatever you get is diluted by close to 99% or more. Strong stuff. But while most of the labels bragged about killing power, when it came to carpenter ants every fogger and sprayer noted the importance of finding the nests. Nests? Nests are for birds.

Rather than make a purchase, I figured a trip home to research carpenter ants on the internet might be a better idea.

Google. Carpenter Ants. Google. Carpenter Ant Nests. A 559,000 search history. A lot of people have ant problems.

The more I read, the less I felt ready to tackle the problem. First, I got the general picture. They don't eat wood. They nest in wood. That's where the damage comes from. That wasn't going to make my sweet wife any happier about living with them. They have a caste system like in India. There's the Queens. That figures. Winged Males. Of course aren't we all. Major Workers. That was easier before the economic crisis. Minor Workers. That's the category Sally would most likely pick for me. I wasn't getting anywhere, especially since the articles all talked about the importance of finding the nests and how difficult that can be.

So I switched to identification versus other bugs. Maybe we didn't have carpenter ants at all. Maybe we just had Visitor Ants and they already had their bags packed, ready to vacation in the great outdoors. I learned to spot the difference between regular ant workers and the more ambitious carpenter ant workers. I wondered if they checked in at the union hall before getting work.

I discovered things about the seasonal habits of carpenter ants. North facing nests stay dormant all winter. South ones have a creepy crawling movement to them year round. I read about how the Queens drop their wings when they're ready to mate. Sounded familiar. Their outside nests usually start in rotting woodpiles and then they make for the hotel where they prefer sugar snacks to anything else.

That was it. Rotting, wet, unattended-for-years kind of wood. I'd been collecting it for over a decade behind the garage right below the new headquarters of the Mullet Lake Carpenter Ant Association, dues optional. My back cabin bedrooms.

It took me no more than a half hour to get to the hardware store again and get back with my super ant killer spray bottle, the one with a handy attachment for mass application in case my adversaries noticed what I was up to and attacked. I would if someone threatened my fancy new digs.

An hour later I was finished. Of course, according to the literature it would take a month to know whether I commanded an effective deterrent to their invasion. In fact, one line haunted me. It said "you may never now if carpenter ants have been completely eradicated." I crossed "Ants" off my list. Next up: "Mice."

Back to the computer.'

Looking for a Five Horse Outboard Motor
Friday, July 10th, 2009

A couple of weeks ago in Columbus, Ohio, my black 240,000 miles-on-it 1998 Jeep Grand Cherokee was stolen. I was in the process of loading things from the self storage unit near our old apartment, the final transfer of possessions we didn't know what to with when we made the move to Cheboygan in early spring. I parked it for the night at a friend's house in a safe neighborhood, but in the morning it was gone. All I could think of for a few confusing seconds was 'where did I put it?' as though the vehicle were car keys and not a car, and the more sublime inquiry, 'how could it just drive off by itself?' thinking my years of calling her Betty had endowed her with the ability to run off for an oil change all by herself.

After renting a car one way and coming home, I heard from a policeman. He asked me if I wanted it towed to someplace other than the Columbus impound lot and that it wasn't drivable. I told him I lived five hundred miles away now and didn't know when I'd be back. My wife and I would be sharing her car for a while, I told him, and he countered that he felt sorry about that and wished me luck.

Without wheels for a while and with a couple of projects finished, I turned to my self appointed duty of making sure everything around our Mullett Lake cottage was in proper working condition; electrics, plumbing, chimney, power tools and the rest of the never ending and always capitalized list of important things I write down and hope to get to but never do. That's mostly because I don't know anything much about how anything works. But I had made a very specific pledge I had to keep, the only promise I made out loud on New Year's Eve of last year… when my sweet, understanding, and "do-what-you-say-you'll-do" wife couldn't hear me. It was 'I will learn to do things myself and fix things myself.'

I wish it had been something different, something about making sure nobody stole my Jeep. Maybe I'd have done something differently like waiting for a parking space in my buddy's courtyard down south instead of settling for a spot around the corner on the street. But no, it had been clearly stated from my very own lips. I had learning to do. I had plenty of unused tools so I started in the garage.

Begin with the simpler things, I whispered to my conscience. Weed Whacker. No, I had no weeds to whack. Maybe the Circular Saw. Possibly. Leaf Blower. No leaves. Snow Blower. Wrong season again. No wait. There it was. Under the boat tarp. The perfect choice for a man stranded while his mate runs errands to Glenn's. The outboard motor. The five horse little beauty I grew up with as a boy on the lakes of northern Minnesota. A handsome, white topped 1961 Evinrude.

It had been a gift from my older brother when he heard we were moving north, something of a homecoming present.

Our wooden Lyman rowboat was licensed and already in the water, hooked to the white buoy in the shallows beside our dock. I had read on the brass emblem riveted on the back inside of the boat that it was rated for up to a nine horse motor. Though I didn't remember a gas tank when my brother dropped off the motor on his way to Florida in the fall, it was the only one in the garage, and the hose clipped into place like it yearned for the partnership. I was in business, and there was plenty of fuel for a good long test ride around the lake to ensure the old girl's readiness for months of service. Maybe I'd do a lot of fishing this year. I needed to learn more about that, too.

After changing into my swim trunks and t-shirt, I lugged the motor and tank to the dock, hopped in the water, and pulled the boat alongside. The sun came out and made the fifty degree water go blue in an instant.

A minute later, with the motor screwed tightly into place and all systems go, I put the throttle on start and pulled the cord. It started like a veteran of a million voyages, the low throated murmur of neutral with bubbles rising up. I grabbed a lifejacket, tightened it up real good, shifted the gear bar, and taxied out past the buoys. I turned the throttle handle all the way to the left, to fast, and skimmed along the perfectly smooth water that reflected crystal stars of sunlight.

With the wind in my hair and faced forward to the ancient wooden prow, I was a sailor from another time. I was pretty darn proud of myself until I heard that awful sound of catastrophic engine failure, the sound of seizing up, a terminal cough, the noise you must hear when the earth stands still, a sudden stopping for all time.

After rowing back to the shore for an hour, I borrowed my wife's car and went into town with the outboard and the fuel tank. At the marina in town, Jerry gave me the bad news.

"This tank doesn't have any oil in it, man. You burned it up."

"Oil?"

"You need about a twenty to one mixture depending on the engine. All these little motors run with oil in the gas."

"My brother gave me the motor and the tank."

"Call your brother."

I did, and Jerry was right. My brother left only the outboard motor as a present figuring I'd get a new one and I'd remember about the oil in the tank, I'd hooked up an old one with no oil in it, one that a guest left years ago.

So I finish this article with a statement of my continued commitment to doing things myself and fixing things myself… as well as this classified ad: Looking for a Five Horse Outboard Motor. Call 1-231-268-3688.

Winterizing Season Approacheth
Friday, July 17th, 2009

O.K. Let's be honest. We're well past the Fourth of July. During the last couple of days, it dawned on me like a two by four to the forehead. Winterize now.

We'd moved to a summer cottage, we didn't have a lot of dough. We had the leaky faucet of summer homes in Cheboygan County. That little guy inside who knows what he's talking about told me cold weather is only four months downstream. My grasshopper days were numbered. Time for action. But what action?

First things first. Plumbing. Pipes freeze at twenty below Fahrenheit. I called the plumber guys and they came right out. As they got out of their truck, they looked like Sherlock Holmes and Dr. Watson in denim work shirts. Following them from room to room, from pump house to the garage, I noticed them shaking their heads, musing about solutions and following leads. Flashlights in their hands, they peered into my crawl space under the cottage, a dark and dangerous Middle Earth. In the bright yellow light of morning, they asked me questions as though I was the only witness to a crime.

"Any insulation in the walls?" said the tall skinny man, the one obviously in charge.

"I don't know. I think so."

"Because there's none under there."

When they drove off, I had a list of recommendations: insulate everything, wrap the pipes in heat tape, and forget using the back cabin in winter because all the pipes run through an unheated garage. Cripes, I said to myself. The laundry room is in the back cabin. I got sudden visions of trips to the laundromat in town through howling blizzards. Sally was not going to be thrilled about this.

After an hour on the World Wide Web, I had a list of things I could tackle on my own. It was one item long. Insulate the attic. An article on Wikipedia pointed me in the right direction. Rent a machine that blows a mixture of recycled newsprint and a bonding material and shoot the stuff into the attic making sure not to get any on the attic ceiling which is the underside of the roof because condensation will soak the stuff and you'll have a real mess. Don't cover the vents at all.

It was clear you had to be a pretty good shot with the nozzle or you could make matters worse. I took the pencil from behind my ear and reluctantly drew a line through my only do-it-yourself scheme. I needed some help. I remembered my mom telling me when I was ten years old 'there's nothing wrong with asking for help' and my mom was always right.

I called my handyman Ken who'd said he needed whatever work he could get this summer and told him I had some things for him to do. He showed up just after dinner.

The wind came up from the northeast and threw our words around the yard like confetti.

"You want me to insulate the crawl spaces and wrap the pipes with heat tape?"

"Right. I'm too big to slide around under there."

"And I go rent the machine for the attic and do that."

"I'll be your assistant on the attic project."

"Okay."

Before Ken left, he did a walkabout through the cottage. He didn't say a word as he looked around, popping his head up through the trap door to the attic, knocking on the pine walls with his ear pressed to the wood, opening and shutting the front and side doors. He stared at the fireplace for a few minutes and then crouched inside the sooty space with his neck and head cranked around like a great curious bird.

Back outside again, he slithered on his back with arms tight to his side through the opening to the crawl space. He looked like a man sneaking back into a prison after a night on the town. He seemed to have trouble for a second like he was pinned down by the house as hard and fast as the wicked witch in Munchkin Land. He rolled over, toes in the dirt, and struggled back out.

On his feet again, he smiled.

"Piece of cake."

"Really?"

"This will be fun."

"Fun?"

I followed him to his truck where he scribbled some things on a coffee stained legal pad. The writing didn't come easily for him. His knuckles were stiff and painful looking and I could tell he was fighting to get his spelling right.

"I'll do it for maybe $200, Mr. Lewis," he said, handing me his notes. "I'll call you tomorrow. Here's a list you won't like."

As his old red pickup disappeared down my gravel road, I put on my reading glasses and studied his scribbles: new doors, new storm doors, fireplace insert, wood burning stove, insulated vinyl siding.

The last one I could barely make out but finally did. Snow Blower.

One Nice Walleye
Friday, July 24th, 2009

When Max, our 24-year old son, arrived at our cottage last Saturday afternoon, he uttered words I'd never heard before.

"Hey Dad, can we go fishing? I bought a license on the way up."

"Sure," I responded with confidence though I have none when it comes to fishing.

For some reason, even with growing up in Minnesota and spending parts of the last twenty summers on the western shore of Mullett Lake, I never found myself comfortable around a tackle box. I bought one when the kids were little, stuffed it full of monofilament line, Lindy lures, needle nose pliers, sinkers, nail clippers, and everything else I could remember from my brother's box when he used to drag me out on the lake back home when we were young.

I'd put it in a closet in the back cabin with the old spinning rods I inherited when we bought our place. My two boys never inquired about it, never once asked to go fishing. They'd been interested in boats and skis and inner tubes and crawfish and girls later on. But never fish. I figured it was natural cause neither was I.

The lake was dark grey like the sky with a stiff northeast breeze kicking into gear. I told Max to throw his things in his room and tell his mom we were going out. As he sauntered out on the dock, I noticed a man's cut to his shoulders and back, a different look than how I remembered him. He lowered our little Lyman skiff from the hoist and pulled it alongside the end deck and secured it. As I passed the kitchen window with a pole rigged up in one hand and my cobwebbed tackle box in the other, Sal smiled encouragement but there was worry on her face though. I knew the look.

Near the side of the cottage, I turned over the round granite rocks lining our flower bed and found three nice nightcrawlers. A good luck sign.

Puttering past the buoy, I handed Max the rod and we trolled for an hour. Through choppy waves, we worked our way along the drop off, checking our bait every ten minutes or so. Our life jackets straps were pennants in the wind, slapping against us, and the spray from small white caps drenched our faces. Not a nibble. Not a bite. Had I rigged it right? Was I using the right spinner? Was the nightcrawler too hapless and thin? I had absolutely no idea.

"Maybe they're just not interested," I said.

"Can we try something else?"

"Something else?"

"You know. From your tackle box."

I opened it up and placed it on the bench seat between us. It was like staring at a map when you can't read. Little packages of hooks and lures, lures, lures. Fluorescent yellows and greens. When I held up a slip bobber, Max nodded his head.

He let the bobber and a newly hooked worm over the side and we drifted back from it. I gave the old Evinrude a little more gas and we stayed in one place long enough to get completely soaked, the bow rising and slapping the water to the rhythm of the bobber.

"This isn't going to work, Max. We'll try in the morning. Tomorrow's supposed to be nice and sunny. I'll go to the Mullett Lake Country Store and get some big Canadian Crawlers."

"Just another minute."

"Sure."

"The bobber's gone, Dad."

"Did it come loose?"

"I don't see it."

The rod tip bent slightly. Then it wiggled and pulled. Then it bent to the water with Max reeling steadily. The little net was too small. It was for trout. The fish moved under the boat with purpose, but that gave me a chance to grab the line and pull it in. It was a good sized walleye. It flopped and began to fight more than it did in the water. I got the hook out easily enough and then realized I didn't have a stringer in the tackle box.

I pinned the fish to the wood planks with both feet after pricking my forefinger on the back fin. I turned the motor and started for shore.

"You O.K., Dad?"

"This is one nice walleye."

"The Birds" of Mullett Lake
Friday, July 31st, 2009

And I thought carpenter ants were the scourge of my summer. Wrong. Now, each morning when I plant my feet on the floor beside my bed and rub the sleep from my eyes, I look down towards the lake and there they are. A crowd of herring seagulls huddling tight together on top of our Shore Station like emperor penguins. Every morning I run down the dock waving my arms as though I'm a giant bird of prey taking flight and they disperse lazily out into the water fifty yards away to await my retreat.

For years, a clan of twenty to thirty determined gulls has been big trouble for my neighbor John, his white metal dock just perfect for them. Cool to their webbed feet. Warm in the sun. Free of stanchions. Shallows teeming with small crawfish. A restaurant and day spa all in one.

Every summer John dutifully washes his dock after he chases them off, swearing as he scrubs at the mess one section at a time. He claims to have tried everything in the seagull fighting handbook. Owl dummies with flapping wings, screeching eagle noise makers, grape based misters, whirligigs of all kinds. But as fate would have it, almost four times as many birds arrived last month while he was gone. Right after a painstaking new paint job and with just weeks to go before hosting his only daughter's big fat lakeside wedding.

Sal and I tried scaring them off by driving our little boat at them over and over, circling madly around the end deck, but to no avail. They'd just hop in the water and look at us like we were crazy people with a broken rudder. The big ones, the great granddaddies of all the rest, didn't move. When John and his family returned, his dock was not the least bit white anymore.

After two days of slave labor with giant brushes and bleach, John and his wife Frankie had their dock looking like new again. He put two chaises out on the end deck, but unfortunately the gulls seemed to appreciate the new furnishings and came back with a vengeance. Then he stood guard all afternoon with a long broom and swung it over his head whenever they swooped in. In a last ditch effort, he took all his heavy lawn furniture to the farthest out sections, turned the chairs upside down, and tightened string around the feet in an enormous Bohemian cobweb. Much to everyone's surprise, it worked.

That's when my troubles started.

First, it was just the big boys. They arrived last week the morning after John erected his masterpiece. Four of them. They were testing out my plastic cover tarp as Roosting Heaven Two. I calmly walked down my dock and barked a shrill "hey' and they took off like they knew I meant business. So much for those guys.

With a persistent rainy day settling in, I took to the keyboard to catch up on work and didn't check on things out on the lake for hours. On my way to the kitchen, I saw them. The same huge flock that had been plaguing John's little pier were perched on my cover. I recognized the biggest one. Grey and confident. John calls him George. One of the advance guard from earlier in the day. There had to be a hundred of his colleagues having a crawfish picnic and talking about how much they like their new place. Better view, too.

I ran down the dock waving a canoe paddle over my head and they reluctantly took to the sky. But the way George soared in great loops above me said they'd be back as soon as I returned to shore. This was going to be a war and I'd have to wage it quickly and effectively. Shock and awe if necessary. These birds were settling in like my nightmares after watching Hitchcock's "The Birds" when I was a kid.

I thought about enlisting John's help but one look at the menacing menagerie at the end of his dock told me to go elsewhere for the right strategy.

A little research on the internet threw a bunch of options at me.

One blog website was devoted to the subject. There was an article about the great success of a duck club in Utah (the seagull is their state bird) that released two weaner pigs on their property.

None of these products got a passing grade from sally, especially the weaner pigs.

I went to the Summer Store in Indian River and bought a loon windmill. I put it up and George and company immediately landed in mass in a strong wind, the whirling waterfowl nothing but a curiosity. I cleaned the entire dock and tarp, fresh as a daisy. More seagulls. They seemed to appreciate the housekeeping.

Tomorrow I plan on staying out there all day in a clown suit if I have to. With the canoe paddle.

My Top Ten Reasons for Moving North
Friday, August 7th, 2009

The other day my friend Chip from Columbus, Ohio called me. He wanted to know how we were doing since we moved to Cheboygan in March. Like every one of the old cadre from down south, whenever they check in with us there's the inevitable "I don't know how you're going to make it through the winter in northern Michigan" sympathy talk, and I heard it from him, too, as though everyone in the world thinks there's no way a city boy like me has a chance to make it through the winter up here. The blizzards, the ice, the long dark nights... my survival skills. I always respond that I grew up in Duluth, but I can sense a disbelieving shaking of heads anyway. They know me too well.

It got me thinking about David Letterman's Top Ten Reasons shtick that's helped make his show so popular over the years. He starts from the number ten and reads his list from ten back to number one, with a drum roll, for ridiculous comic effect. The call made me want to do the same. Apologies to the master. My Top Ten Reasons for Moving Up North:

10. I took out a huge mortgage on the lake cottage based on house values in 2005 to buy out my relatives. Everybody on the planet knows the math in 2009 on that one! Dumped the down state mortgage in the process. Now it's one place, one payment Better odds.

9. I haven't had to wait in traffic since we moved except for a very short older lady in a 1989 Pontiac on the two lane blacktop of the South Straits Highway. She had her left blinker on for a good mile as she puttered along towards Wal-Mart at about twenty miles an hour. The blinker was comforting, not aggravating.

8. A good breakfast here is religion, not some recommendation from the National Institute of Health. It's not granola and vitamins. It's eggs, potatoes and a little meat. Stack of toast.

7. The customer service difference between "I don't know, maybe" and "you betcha."

6. Snow banks come in Brilliant White, not Exhaust Pipe Dirt or Road Salt Grey.

5. A heat wave means a day in the eighties Fahrenheit, not weeks in the nineties or the hundreds (though since the summer solstice this year we've had exactly zero heat waves).

4. The nasty biting, whining-in-your-ear mosquito season lasts about a month. With a little rain in Ohio, five months.

3. New cars up north look just like my two old ones (almost 500,000 odometer miles between them) when a little gravel road dust is thrown on them.

2. If the refrigerator looks empty you can grab a fishing rod, shotgun or rifle depending on the season. Of course you have to know how to use them.

1. Sally is deliriously happy.

Do They Snarl and Bare Their Teeth?
Friday, August 14th, 2009

Even though I rented a splitter a couple of months ago and stacked what I thought was enough birch to last us through the winter, the wood is half gone. Some summer we've had. Had a fire going in the fireplace most nights since the Fourth of July to keep the electric heat bill to a minimum.

Over coffee, I told Sally that we'd have to order wood after all.

"Why don't you hike along the trail every day and pick up a little fallen timber on the way back?" she asked. "You need the exercise and we don't have the money. After a month we'll have plenty of wood."

"A month?"

"Yup. Walk a mile south and a mile back. When you get close to home, pick up an armful. It's all over the place."

"You don't think I can do it, do you?"

"Yes I do. And you don't have a choice. We need wood. Your last two job interviews didn't go anywhere."

An hour later, dressed in my heavy old jeans and a long sleeved t-shirt with leather work gloves sticking out of my hip pocket, I started down the North Central State Trail that passes right behind our place on Mullett Lake. My clothes meant I was serious about doing this; exercise then hard labor. I was prepared. Nothing could stand in the way of success on my thirty day mission of getting in shape and laying in wood for the winter. Not mosquitoes or sand flies. Not poison oak or poison ivy. Not scratches or cuts or bruises.

First, the exercise. I began with a pretty good stride, enjoying the rise of an orange red sun over the still waters of the lake. Crows were cawing, surprised to find me on the old Gaylord to Cheboygan route. After a half mile, I started dragging my feet along the crushed limestone. Sally was absolutely right. I needed to do this more for my health than the fuel. I picked up the pace even though I was starting to sweat profusely. It had to be the hottest day of summer. Really humid.

When I reached Long Point, I turned around and began my return hike, walking with half the steam of the outward mile.

I'd never used the trail much. Slowing down let me gaze down the tunnel of overhanging poplar, birch, and bent cedars. Sunlight like tiny stars sprinkled the path. I'd read about the conversion of the old Michigan Central Railroad lines into one of the finest summer hiking and biking trails on the planet and one of best snowmobile runs in the state.

A breeze from the south picked up and pushed at my lazy back side. My confident, easy stride returned.

Near the Grand Resort not far from home base, I began sizing up the right pieces of dead and dry hardwoods to carry the rest of the way. I planned on being very selective. I put on my gloves and stepped off the trail a few feet. 'Here's one.' I carried it another fifty yards. 'Here's another.'

The day was getting hotter by the second. I heard myself breathing heavily for the first time. Then I heard the sound of something following me deeper off the path. When I took a step, a creature moved with me. When I stopped abruptly, so did my stalking companion. Peering into a dreamlike sea of green branches where I sensed it was, I waited for movement. I suddenly wished I could see like I could when I was younger. What does a coyote look like? Are they aggressive? Do they slink along when seeking their prey? Have they ever attacked a two legged adversary? Do they growl, snarl, or bare their teeth before they strike?

A giant black squirrel abruptly stood up on his hind legs. I dropped my three trophy logs onto the trail, just missing my right big toe. The squirrel didn't move. He or she seemed to be smiling at me, ready to spit out his mouth full of pine nuts and unleash a real belly laugh.

I gathered my logs and grabbed a couple of other more imperfect ones and started for the cottage. Back at the leaning tower of garages I call my wood shed, I put them where they belonged.

Sally walked out the kitchen door waving big thumbs up.

"You made it." She cheered. "It took you a long time to go two miles. You're drenched."

"Good exercise," I said walking past her on the way to the shower upstairs. "Good wood."

On the Job Training for Job Hunting
Friday, August 21st, 2009

When Sally and I started making plans three years ago for selling almost everything we owned, including our old money pit house in Ohio, and moving to the north country full time, we missed the mark on a couple of essential things.

First by a long shot was thinking our savings would be a status quo deal. We'd even dreamt it would be a bigger nest egg by the time we got here last March. Unfortunately, we were as wrong on that one as Alan Greenspan was in his rose colored belief that sub prime loans were good for America.

In second place, but not by much, was the idea that our copious experience in business, communications, and professional writing would lead us to new jobs of some kind in our fields. We figured downsizing in income was naturally part of it. That comes with a lower cost of living. But the work would be there nonetheless. We used our Monster membership and sent out a hundred queries.

Zero. Zip. Zilch.

So we had a team meeting the other morning right after the night when five inch rains and thunderstorms pummeled our cottage into leaky submission. Over the strongest black coffee, we stared at each other like Bobby Fisher and Boris Spassky in their legendary chess showdown in Iceland long ago.

"I've got a bunch of interviews lined up," I offered.

"I sent my resume to the bookstore people yesterday," Sal answered.

My first stop was the Michigan Works office. Great people doing a great job. I was a bit of a strange bird, but they recognized a worthy challenge when they saw one and signed me up for a retraining orientation. They sent me off with a stack of job leads I had no idea were out there.

I decided to exhaust my own two prospects before attacking the state's list of opportunities.

I stopped at a downtown store my editor suggested might need some help. I hustled over to Wal-Mart and spent time at the electronic employment kiosk.

The new job leads pulled me up Route 23 to Mackinaw City. It was a hot, hazy day and the winds were mighty from the south, buffeting my car on my way towards the bridge. Buck up, I said to myself.

'Night desk attendant. New Resort, Year- round.' I filled out the paperwork while imagining cold lonely nights in January waiting for guests.

'Retail sales position at Crossroads. Experience preferred.' I'd certainly bought enough stuff there. Would that qualify? I scratched my signature on the application.

There were four job notices for late season hotel staff on Mackinac Island so I hopped on a brand new boat at Shepler's Dock and did the math on the fare. Fifteen minute ride over and fifteen back. Fifteen buck ticket. Fifty cents a minute. My mind was wandering as the prow of the craft smashed great waves out of the way like they weren't there. Before I knew it, I was strolling around eating fudge, my hair standing on end from the high humidity and gusty breeze. I applied for three positions but passed on the fourth when a very nice man with big hands and a dark tan described the duties of the horse attendant. It involved a special shovel.

Back on the mainland on a park bench along North Huron Avenue, I thumbed through more help wanted postings.

'General laborer for year round work on Bois Blanc Island. Knowledge of logging practices required.' I put that one back in the folder I carried with me, the one with twenty neatly polished and customized resumes I'd prepared for any type of job situation I'd run into. I had one for management and administration and one for sales and marketing. There was a service master resume and another highlighting my communications and writing pedigree.

I started back to the cottage after finishing the fudge and sucking the melted chocolate from my fingers.

As I neared the turn off to Silver Beach Road on Mullett Lake, I pulled over. Sally was retrieving some letters from our highway mailbox and placing an envelope and a small package inside for pickup. I waved and she got in.

"What are you mailing out?"

"My manuscript. My agent really liked the first chapter," she replied with a smile. "And the bookstore people want to see my transcripts from college."

"They called you?"

"Yes they did. But they said they have a ton of applicants. They'll be calling people for interviews next week."

"Terrific."

"How'd you do?"

"I met a lot of nice people and took care of my sweet tooth."

Off to My Old Home Town
Friday, August 28th, 2009

This past weekend Sally and I drove a neighborly nine hours from Cheboygan to Duluth, Minnesota, my old home town full of relatives, old friends, and my still chugging along rather ancient parents. We were off to my brother's oldest boy's wedding and started out on Thursday into a soup of steady rain. The thick ground-hugging fog surprised me. A big easterly tossed twigs and last year's leaves around our gravel driveway like so much confetti. Before we were out on the Straits Highway, Sally had pulled over.

"You drive. The bridge scares me in a wind."

I got behind the wheel.

Halfway across the bridge I was glad to be driving since Sally had her eyes squeezed as tight as a fist in a street fight. Vehicles moved like turtles on a beach. Mackinac Island was invisible. So was the water below. The car shook violently enough to make me forget about the toll. I passed through the manned booth on the far right side without paying. I had to back up and fumble through my pockets for three bucks as Sally asked me if I was all right. I wasn't.

I was thinking about our windshield wipers flapping madly all the way through the U.P., northern Wisconsin and on to the head of the Lakes. I saw images of the inevitable endless stretches of two lane blacktop with thousands of orange barrels and slow moving RV's. But that wasn't the real problem. It was leaving behind so much unfinished business at Mullett Lake with autumn right around the bend that worried me more than the wet shrouded pavement. The idea of not being ready for winter and the future we'd dreamed was a bigger threat.

"I know what you're thinking, Don. Give it up for a few days," she insisted. "For my sake enjoy your family."

"How did you know what I'm thinking?"

"Try thirty years together. Just drive."

By the time we reached our favorite lunch place in Munising on Lake Superior, I was free of the ghosts of winters yet to come. With a charbroiled California burger on the plate below me, the smell of onions and charcoal all around me, the glorious phantoms of my childhood appeared instead. I saw myself slamming opponents into the boards in a big championship hockey game. I heard my uncle tell me it was OK that my dad didn't understand me (I was twenty years old at the time). I felt the bottoms of my feet hurt when I thumped the bottom of the upper bunk where my ten year old brother slept just to make him mad.

Next stop, Marquette. Then Iron River, Wakefield, Ashland, Superior, and finally the cabin in Twig, Minnesota. At Grand Lake, despite endless bills and crises we kids never recognized, my parents had made perfect summer on the lake for my brother and sisters and me.

The wedding magnified my understanding of incredibly good fortune. I could see in the eyes of my nephew Freddie and his bribe Rebecca that love has a chance to conquer all. Sally hung on my arm and danced with me on a parquet floor at the old club in front of a less than super talented DJ who played "Stand by Your Man." My mom, at 85, did the same. I hugged my best friend from thirty years ago who'd been through huge troubles with his own family and then watched him break dance on the slippery surface in front of me while I clapped until my hands were beet red. My dad, not exactly straight up in his wheel chair, refused to leave knowing he might not see such joy surrounding his bloodline again. My sisters and I seemed like planets orbiting the same sun. And later that night I took a sauna with my weary brother and stared at Jupiter and Mars in a moonless night sky on our old dock.

The ride back to the Straits of Mackinac the next day was mostly silent. I guess I'd call it a perfect silence.

Girls' Weekend
Friday, September 4th, 2009

In every man's life there's a girls' weekend. I'm talking about when your significant other, your sometimes forgiving wife who puts up with your bad habits and rambling dissertations on a regular basis, decides the entire upcoming Friday through Sunday Night slot of your short life belongs to her, her best friends, her sister, my nieces, and for good measure all the females of the world.

It's not that I was banished last weekend when everyone arrived. No orders from Sal that I play thirty six holes of golf or embark on that all day solo I'd been talking about. There wasn't a hint of 'why don't you' in her words. No, it was simpler than that.

"You're going to be miserable," she informed me as she made her way to the back cabin with a load of fresh linens for her soon-to-arrive entourage.

"I love your sister. I'll stay out of the way. My projects list has mushroomed lately."

"I'm telling ya, you're going to be miserable."

"I'll ask Derek and his wife to come over for a picnic on Saturday. "

Derek's my hunting buddy. He works for the DNR. Grouse season wasn't far off so it seemed a logical idea.

"No you won't."

Since we moved from Ohio earlier in the year, Sal hadn't laid eyes on her sister or any of her best friends from down south. We've made a host of new friends in northern Michigan but these were the women who still knew her best and her struggles with all the transition in our lives. I put up no argument.

When our cottage property filled with excitement and long overdue hugs, I did my best to stay out of the way. But what can you do when there's a platter full of smoked salmon, five kinds of cheese and my favorite crackers on a table surrounded by happiness in lawn chairs. You get in and you get out. You do it again. You do a few chores. You wait and you wait for signs that dinner might be underway. You make another move for the appetizers. You listen to everyone catching up and you realize you're miserable and invisible at the same time.

I went upstairs to bed early on Friday night after making a roaring birch wood fire for the girls. But even with my white noise machine blasting 'Crashing Waves in Carmel' into the night, I heard below me the kind of laughing and clinking of glasses usually reserved for a New Year's Eve party or when your team finally makes the NFL playoffs. I used my time in bed wisely.

I made an imaginary chalkboard of the darkness. On it in bold I scheduled two days jammed full of the great outdoor adventures I'd been putting off because there was clear consensus in our abode that looking for employment and buttoning up our former summer-only cottage for its first winter as real shelter took precedence. By the time I dozed off I had almost too many options. A full morning of fishing in our little skiff out on the lake. A very leisurely afternoon bike ride south along Mullett Lake to the Sturgeon River Valley, scouting good places to try fly fishing. A cold beer in Wolverine. A stop on the way back in Topinabee at Breaker's for one of their super hot pizzas. I planned to arrive at dusk back at our place; exhausted, satisfied and a hero as far as Sally was concerned just for bugging out all day.

Saturday morning a rain settled in that you couldn't see through. If there's such a thing as a thousand percent humidity, that was it. The forecast had called for intermittent light rain showers. I'd put a light poncho in the day pack for the bike ride and was prepared for a little moisture but this was ridiculous. At my computer before the girls rose for breakfast, I had a staring contest with the National Weather Radar that showed a gigantic, hurricane-looking thing swirling over the Mackinac Straits, unwilling to budge. I blinked first.

Now what? Write all day. Where? I heard rumors the night before that if the girls encountered a serious rainy day there'd be a Chick Flick Festival in the living room.

With a towel over my head, I slogged through my swampy yard to the laundry room and on through to the garage with my laptop in a plastic garbage bag inside my raincoat and tucked under my arm. I made a second trip with the coffeemaker we'd retired when we got the new one.

Every man needs two offices. One for regular days and one for Girls' Weekend.

Someone is Stealing Docks
Friday, September 11th, 2009

On Tuesday, the day after Labor Day, I gathered the new job ads from all the Northern Lower Peninsula Michigan newspapers, sent out my material, and made calls. During the afternoon I climbed the mountainous hills west of home in the old Volvo and filled out more applications than a single pen full of ink could handle. A guy named Alec asked me to meet him about an open, commission-only sales position after dinner at a little restaurant in Harbor Springs so I arrived back at our cottage after dark, a nearly full waning moon hanging high in the night sky. I was tired and went to bed quickly after Sally made me a dinner of sweet corn on the cob, salad, and leftover pork chops.

Early in the morning I walked out the front door towards the lake. Through a shroud of fog trying to mask the sunrise, I noticed neighbor John's dock was missing. To the north towards town four other docks had disappeared, their boat lifts standing naked and embarrassed out in the water. Had thieves used the full moon to sneak through yards, dismantle the docks, and carry them away?

No. It was time for the dreaded ritual and I knew it. I hung my head thinking Sally must have watched the section by section process the day before knowing full well it marked the retreat of our close friends along Mullett Lake back below the 45th parallel. I was glad she slept in... or so I thought.

She was right behind me.

"Someone is stealing the docks," I said stoically. "The boat lifts will be next."

"Buck up. We made this decision together."

"The maple leaves are coming down."

"I know. Doesn't that mean grouse to you or something like that?"

"Well, actually, yes."

Had I been so busy with winterizing our cottage and finding a job that I hadn't focused for a second on two of my favorite things: grouse and duck hunting?

I took the day off. I called my DNR pal Derek from Indian River, caught him on his way back from his station in the U.P., and invited him over for dinner the following weekend. I met him in the woods last fall, someplace deep in the Cheboygan State Forest and we hunted partridge and mallards together a bunch of times after that.

Next I cleared out our garage full of stuff from down south, the things always left in boxes after a move. I found what I was looking for. I found the waders. I pulled out my shotgun case, my duffel with shells and the orange vest. My boots, my cleaning kit, my Thermos, my compass were all intact.

Then I spied them under a pile of winter coats and boots in a big plastic bin: my old hockey skates. I saw another way to face the coming months. I figured I'd glide across the ice on the lake after it freezes and before the snow arrives. Later I could keep my momentum going during public skating on the Zamboni made surface at the Ice Arena. I played Division I hockey long ago. I was a pretty good defenseman. I could look into the youth program and see if any coaches needed help.

In a box of books I found the National Audubon Society Field Guide to Weather that son Max gave me last Christmas. Sitting on a broken chair designated for the dump, I read about Arctic Air Masses, a rarity even in northern Michigan in the middle of winter.

Something about the Coreolis Force, the effect of the earth's rotation on low pressure troughs and high pressure ridges. For the most part it keeps the really cold stuff north of Hudson's Bay.

I heard Sally yelling for me about noon time. The day was getting hot, maybe the second or third day the whole summer with sweat involuntary when you stood directly in the sun. I could hear only two words. "Buoy time!"

For some reason, I jogged out of the garage feeling younger than when I entered. I felt my heart beat as though the next day and the next day would be an adventure, not a worry. At the end of the dock we slipped into the perfectly glassy water. A washed out orange Tide bottle under Sal's arm would be our marker for finding the spot next spring. Chest deep in the lake by the cement blocks, I dove under the azure surface and grabbed the heavy chinks of chain lying inches deep in the sand. Holding my breath as I attached the bottle halfway down, I felt like Mike Nelson (Lloyd Bridges) in the 1960's TV show Sea Hunt.

When I surfaced, Sally was laughing. With one hand holding the buoy, she pointed at a bald eagle swooping across our inlet with a fish in its talons.

"What's so funny?" I asked as I started to giggle in odd harmony with her.

"Look where we are. Look at the eagle."

A Letter Found in an Old Trunk
Friday, September 18th, 2009

This past weekend I received an email from a stranger on the west coast. She inquired about a letter she discovered in an old trunk decades ago. The woman, Conradine, explained that her love of exploring the past led her to a career in set design for theatre and movies, including for Disney. She specializes in the 1800's and early

1900's. She was doing research on the letter after finding it tucked away in her attic. The letter was dated May 29, 1925, and the masthead read Hotel Top-in-a-bee. The great library of the internet led her to my Tribune column from this past spring featuring the elegant Mullett Lake resort's history, the one about my daydreams (if that's what they were) of well-to-do guests from the '20s disembarking from launches for their summer vacations. She sent a scanned copy as an attachment.

Through a flurry of electronic notes, I agreed to receive the original and bring it down to the Topinabee Library a few miles south of our cottage.

The letter was not very cordial. In fact, I found it a rather stern response to a young girl's inquiry about summer work on the dining room staff at the Hotel. There were preemptive admonishments 'if you are planning a summer vacation and not expecting to do any more work than you can help don't bother to answer (this letter) as we have applications coming in every day and can take our pick of the girls this year.' There were questions about her true age. It was written by the son of the owner, one J.E. Bailey.

The last sentence leapt out at me because I'm newly out in the job market just as this young lady was eighty four years ago. 'We are paying $25.00 per calendar month this year, board and room and R.R. fare one way if it does not exceed $6.00.'

I had to show this to Sally. I found her at the kitchen table reading the literature on wood burning stoves I brought home the day before.

"Wow," she said after I quoted the letter, "25 five bucks a month." She didn't look up. "I wonder how much that is in today's money?"

"I have no idea."

"Why don't you figure it out? It's a perfect puzzle for you," she said. "Quit with the yard work for a while. It's going to be October in a week or so."

"I'll get my calculator."

"Do it in your office. And by the way, we're going out tonight. We've had leftovers four straight days and I didn't make it to the store."

I settled into my chair in front of my computer and got to work. First, how many hours a day did dining staff girls work at The Hotel Top-in-a-bee? I figured the number at 12. There are seven days in a week. Thirty and a half days in a month considering 30 days in June and September and 31 for July and August. It was a four-month appointment. I multiplied the numbers by each other one by one and got a total. I divided $25 by that number to make the answer in dollars and cents. I double checked my assumptions. The girl was applying for a job paying just under ten cents an hour.

Next up: the inflation factor. After an hour of Google searches I finally ran across a graph showing a scale I could understand, real world examples contrasting the price of a Ford Model T in 1925 ($300) versus today's Ford Taurus ($25,000). There was a comparison using a loaf of bread and another with the cost of a doctor's visit. Using a little more sixth grade math, I came up with a reasonable answer.

If my young and hopeful girl from down south was applying for the job today she'd be looking at $1.29 an hour.

I looked out the open window of the room I call an office. The afternoon was slipping away though the day's warmth lingered. The skies were cloudless blue, and shadows from our pines and maples stretched across the yard. Stacks of insulating foam called Polar Wrap stared back at me. Piles of vinyl siding did the same. I thought about the estimates I'd gotten for the wood stove and the six cords of wood for stoking it through the winter. I remembered the numbers for a backup generator and the crawl space work.

When I pictured the young girl heading off on the train to her new summer job in the north, I thought about all the reasons I needed work and decided whatever job I took I'd be making pretty good money after all.

We are Year-rounders
Friday, September 25th, 2009

For those who follow my column I'm pleased to report that I'm finally working again. It's part time but a great job with a wonderful and historic downtown Cheboygan company. The people are a real team and the work is challenging as well as interesting. As legendary radio man Paul Harvey would have said... "and now for the rest of the story."

When I got back from my first day on the job, I parked the old Volvo and saw our giant maple trees stirring in a fall wind, sending their leaves all over the yard. Pink ice clouds stretched over the sky reflecting the setting sun. It was warm for September and a dozen fishing boats were gathered off Dodge Point in search of perch.

The smell of fried fish and hash browns knocked me over as I opened our new and rather expensive front storm door.

"I'm home," I hollered in a familiar and hopeful way.

"Wait. I'll be down in a second," Sally yelled down the stairs. The pine walls of our cottage on Mullett Lake had an echo effect I'd never heard before. Over dinner she said how wonderful she felt about the onset of fall. "I'm so glad you got the job."

When we finished eating we went over the things she'd have to handle for me now that most of my day was blanketed with regular work responsibilities.

One: Wood stove. She grabbed all the paperwork including the contract.

Two: Crawl space insulation. A swipe of her hand and the file was gone. Slivers of sunlight shot through the kitchen window and caught the edge of her wedding ring.

Three: Electrician quote. This one I hated giving up.

"The water doesn't move unless we have juice," I said. The look on her face told me to get her the man's number from my cell phone.

"Don't worry. I'll find a cheap generator in the Classifieds or on Craig's List," she answered.

Four: Somebody to plow our driveway, maybe the whole road. She stopped me.

"I'll call Linda and just figure it out. None of this is rocket science." Linda's our neighbor three houses down who settled into a four season life here a while back, running her business from her house on the shore. "Don't worry about this stuff and enjoy the new job. Now give me the whole file."

"O.K."

"Don, I know we're going year round."

At my desk a few minutes later, I thought about what she was trying to get across. It was simple. If I'm not fearful, she's not either. She's perfectly capable of running the homestead. We're year-rounders now. No looking back. Our friends here are more important than neighbors are in the big city. We'll do just fine.

Then it dawned on me. Sally'd also given me the term I'd been searching for to describe what we are. We're Year-rounders. It was perfect. One click on Dictionary.com confirmed it.

Year-rounders [yeer-round-ders] noun. 1. people who are year round residents, as at a seasonal resort. 2. things that are designed for use throughout the year.

As far as the first definition was concerned: close enough. After all, the Grand Resort on Mullett is just a quarter mile down the Straits Highway. Of course no one in their right mind would call our little cottage a resort.

The second definition was accurate as it was troubling. Our place was unquestionably not designed for use throughout the year.

Out my window, Sally sat reading in a chair on the lawn like she always does after dinner. With evening light retreating more each day, we were eating earlier so she could enjoy her passion outdoors a bit longer. I joined her and told her how thankful I was about her stepping up to the plate on all the construction stuff and for giving me a term I could use about settling into the North Country full time.

"We are Year-rounders, Sal."

"You're welcome."

Changing Stripes
Friday, October 2nd, 2009

When you move from one state to another there's a gigantic pile of things you have to do like getting a new driver's license, new car insurance, new health insurance and so on. The health insurance one can be a calamity. Preexisting conditions come into play, so does your age. It's like trying to get good life insurance on your eightieth birthday. It's a hazard facing anyone going from summer resident from Ohio to a full fledged year-rounder in Michigan.

The whole country's talking about health care reform right now and this business about not being able to take your insurance from one state to another obviously tops my list of suggestions to our friends in Washington.

I discovered another "must do" this past weekend.

Sally made her first trip back to Columbus since April. Her dad, Pandel Savic, was getting inducted into the Ohio State Athletics Hall of Fame. He quarterbacked the team to victory in OSU's first Rose Bowl in 1950 and held some records for a while before the Big Ten started throwing the ball in earnest in the 1990s. There was a big banquet and a ceremony at half time of the game against Illinois.

I couldn't go. I'd just started my new job. A couple of days by myself on Mullett Lake loomed as I pulled her suitcase behind me towards her car.

"Drive carefully."

"I will."

"Watch out for deer. They're starting to move around."

The early morning sunlight slipped through the cedars and splashed across her face. She gave me a look I recognized.

"Take it easy this weekend," she said. "You deserve it. Catch a couple of football games. Remember to look for my dad on the field. Game's at 3:00."

With unblinking eyes I followed her car as it turned the corner past our neighbor John's ancient hedges and disappeared. For minutes I stood still as a statue. A blue jay flew past my ear. A couple of chipmunks stopped at my feet, their mouths stuffed with winter meals. After ten minutes a quick breeze came off the water and chilled me out of the daydream. I sauntered back to the cottage for more coffee.

As I poured another cup I realized what had frozen me in place in the driveway. She'd ordered me to watch sports on TV. I hadn't watched a whole game of any kind for over a year though I followed my usual favorites through the print press.

When I got up Saturday morning I made two fried eggs and a huge stack of heavily buttered toast. It was almost eleven o'clock. I'm usually up at dawn. I plopped on the couch and opened the TV This Week magazine from the Tribune. I picked out the games I wanted to see.

By midnight my coffee table was covered with dirty plates and empty beer bottles. Twelve straight hours of gridiron battles and pigskin wars. Four of the top ten rated teams going down to defeat. I felt like a college kid alone in his dormitory room for the first time, the refrigerator all his. But something was bothering me as I cleaned up. When I climbed into bed I knew what had me in a quandary. During the OSU game I'd kept flipping channels to check on Wolverines and Spartans highlights. I almost missed seeing Sal's dad on the field.

Sunday brought the same mysterious conversion. I grew up in Duluth rooting for the Vikings but I knew the Lions were facing a must win to right a long sinking ship. Nineteen straight losses for cripes sake. I liked their new quarterback Matt Stafford. Brett Farve was still a Packer as far I was concerned.

I watched every second of the game in Ford Field. I held my breath as the Redskins came to life. I danced around the ragged old Persian rug in our living room with our Jack Russell terrier over my head when the Lions finally prevailed.

When Sally got back an hour later, I gave her a huge hug.

"So how was your weekend?" she asked.

"Great!"

"Great?"

I told her why. Something important had been taken care of while she was gone, a key "must do" I'd missed completely when we moved up north. I'd needed to root for the home team. It felt terrific I told her. Her smile said she understood, that she knew our lake cottage was becoming a real home in a way it had not been before.

More than a Convenience
Friday, October 9th, 2009

Early last spring, as freshman year-rounders, Sally and I started thinking about the nearest store for the future occasion of two foot snowfalls and northwest winds cruising out of Manitoba and Ontario straight at our Mullett Lake cottage. At least I was. We were walking the wooded hills across the Straits Highway fruitlessly looking for Morel mushrooms. The aspen trees were showing their first hint of leaves. It wasn't much over forty degrees, our breath visible in the damp morning air.

"I sure wish Frank's was still open," I whined. During all our summers on the lake, almost twenty of them, there'd been a small country store operating on the corner by Mullett Village. It closed last year. Our nearest loaf of bread or six pack of beer was now either in Cheboygan or Topinabee. Not that far really, but not convenient either.

"Yeah. What bad luck," she said, taking a detour off the path to search along a low soggy spot.

"I'm just thinking about this winter."

"I know you are but you're worrying about things we can't do anything about."

"Right."

We worked our way along a ridge towards the gas line clearing. No mushrooms. It started to drizzle then it poured. We pulled the hoods of our rain jackets over our heads and plodded towards Polish Line Road and the easy walk downhill back to Route 27.

As we neared the intersection, the rain let up. We heard the crack and whack of hammers and pry bars. We cut across the brown grasses towards the old store. Pieces of two by four and split pieces of plywood were flying out two open doors as though an angry bear was ripping things apart, upset to find no food in the pantries. We approached with caution.

I poked my head inside and saw a pile of rubble where the cash register used to be. A big, young man with muscled arms stood in the cold semi-darkness, hands on hips, taking a minute's rest. We startled him when I said hello. He climbed over the mess and wiped his hands on a rag so he could shake our hands.

"I'm Bob. Bob MacGregor."

Sally and I introduced ourselves and stepped inside his construction nightmare as the rain began again. Bob explained that his whole clan had pooled their resources, stared down the bank that owned the old building, and took the plunge. They were reopening the store.

"When do think you'll be in business, Bob?" Sally asked, looking around.

"By the Fourth of July. The liquor license will take longer, though. But we'll get it."

An older guy with a day's growth of grey beard appeared out of a back room.

"This is my dad, you guys. Bob Sr."

The old man smiled, shook his head, and told us he was crazy to do what they were doing.

"What do you mean?" I asked.

"I had life pretty well figured out. Now I'm back in the water over my head. But what the heck."

Young Bob told us more about their plans. They were renovating the whole place but using a lot of the equipment left behind by the previous owners. The whole family, his wife and kids and his mom and Dad, would be living upstairs and working at the store.

"We'll have fresh pizzas, ribs, all kinds of dinners to go. Ice cream. You name it."

Sally grabbed me by the arm.

"These guys have work to do."

We said our goodbyes and crossed the highway to the bike path along the lake. Back at our place I threw a few logs into our great stone fireplace and put a match to some birch bark to get it going. I remember my deep sense of relief.

The Mullett Village Country Store is fully open now, their license stamped and sealed from Lansing and ready for hunting season.

As Sally and I agreed last night, it's not a convenience store to us. It's a survival store.

Sally's Single Melancholy
Friday, October 16th, 2009

There's only one thing Sally's shared with me about feeling lonely. We were working together stacking ten cords of hardwood dumped in our yard last Sunday. The sun was bright as I've ever seen it, the wind gusty and determined. Leaves were flying across the yard and out onto the waters of Mullett Lake. Our pile of wood just wouldn't diminish no matter how many trips back and forth we made to our selected repository between and under the cedars not far from the kitchen door. The wood burning stove goes in next week.

"I just miss Barb, that's all."

"I do, too."

"Not the way I do."

She was right. Most spring, summer and early fall nights at six o'clock she'd spent an hour with Barb to decompress. Living with me and my indelible worries takes a toll. I'm quick to deny it but it's true. With Barb around she'd have a drink and spill her guts. She'd come home and make me dinner.

Barb lives alone. She's a handsome woman with a sharp sense of humor and a beguiling no nonsense purity about her. She gets her hair done once a week, a ritual of youthful forward thinking I admire. Her daughter and son-in-law, Kate and Robb, break away from their jobs and come up every few weeks during the promise of summer. We all go out to dinner, separate checks, and laugh and tease each other. Kate and Robb and Barb have become incredibly close friends.

Back in the late 1960s Barb moved to Cheboygan from down state. She followed her husband when he got a job at the old forge, now long closed. Fifty years ago Barb and her husband bought the house two doors south from us, put the kids in the Cheboygan schools and settled into their new life. She says it wasn't easy when her husband got sick and didn't make it. I remember how she put it to us one night last summer. 'There we were. A new mortgage. No income,' she said with a wave of her hand and a sly smile. 'But big deal. Everybody faces something like that. You move on.'

Sal's mom died at very young age when our kids were still crashing around on Big Wheels in our neighborhood in Columbus. Barb's the closest thing to a mom she's experienced since then.

Barb's what I call a "long-hauler." She's here from mid-May until the first hard frost. Now Sally has only the migrating birds out her window and the mink that scramble along our shore for daytime company. And only me at night. The other neighbor Year-rounders up and down the dockless bay of Mullett come and go on business. We try to get together whenever they settle in for a while. But Barb's gone until next year.

"Holy cow." I breathed in and out as I rested on the broken, white straight-backed wooden chair I'd dragged from the deck before we started the wood-stacking. The job was bigger than I thought it would be.

"Get off your butt and keep going. You'll stiffen up and we'll never get this done."

Sal had another interview coming up on Thursday. It's a teaching job in St. Ignace. Barb called last Friday to ask how she was doing, to tell her to 'go get 'em' regarding the position. Those were words I couldn't say because I knew she'd think it my usual pep talk. I was lucky enough to be working again. I thanked the sun and stars and the fates and God for Barb calling her like that all the time.

I demonstrated to Sal my expertise in arranging 16 inch pieces on a slight down hill slope. Three pieces of maple one way, three logs across the other. Center breaks. End breaks. Fill up the spaces between. No higher than your neck.

I sat down for a good five minutes and watched Sally methodically handle two logs at a time as she finished one whole section.

"Sal," I said as I got up stretching out my back muscles. "I miss Barb's deviled eggs."

She made two more trips from the woodpile to the stack and stopped.

"Barb handed down secrets to me before she left. I'll make you some eggs when we put a dent in this mountain of wood."

The Cheboygan Daily Tribune Columns

He Walks Through Trees
Friday, October 23rd, 2009

I have trouble keeping up with Derek when we hunt grouse. He's almost 30 years younger and the age difference would be apparent pretty quick in a foot race. I'm 6'4" with a few extra pounds and more grey hair than brown. Derek's eight inches shorter and hungry looking. He walks the woods in the U.P. every day marking trees, denoting sections for harvesting on behalf of the Forestry Department of the DNR. I grind away in front of a desk top. Hunting birds together I always walk the old seasonal logging trails while he takes to the thickets of young aspen, sapling maples and thorny underbrush.

Last weekend my friend Robb and I got off to a late start for hunting with Derek after stopping to get Robb his small game license. Sally and I were really glad Kate and Robb had come up at the last minute for some getaway time. They'd been fighting a huge battle of life changes down state near Detroit. We stayed up late the night before celebrating Sally finally getting the teaching job she was after.

At the Park and Ride lot in Indian River, we switched our gear into Derek's red Jeep. We headed towards the eastern edge of Le Grande Ranch. A mist lingered in the rare warmth of October and Derek turned on his wipers. Robb sat silent in the back listening to Derek recount how many birds he'd seen the last time he'd hunted the ranch. Derek's English Springer spaniel Harley yelped and whined the whole way in anticipation.

After Derek parked beside what few people would call a road, we donned our blaze orange vests, loaded our guns, and formed a three-man line with me in the middle. Harley started working back and forth through heavy cover. Two grouse flushed right away but we couldn't see them through the leaves. We walked a couple miles. More birds, still no shots. With Derek to my right and Robb to my

42

left, I walked down the sandy rutted trail. Harley kept working but he was frustrated with us for not knocking grouse from a gray sky barely visible through the overhanging blanket of red and yellow.

I'd hunted with Derek many times since I met him in the woods of the Cheboygan State Forest. I remember fighting the currents of the Pigeon River one day last year. We were in Derek's canoe paddling our butts off in the early morning dark trying to get to the right spot for setting up a duck blind where the stream makes a marsh leading into Mullett Lake. It was the first time I'd allowed myself more hope than dread about turning my comfortable life upside down in order to hang onto the cottage.

Robb joined me on the road when Derek and Harley disappeared around a beaver pond flooding our path. The acrid but sweet smell of autumn filled my nostrils. To the north stood the greatest stand of beech trees I'd ever seen.

"This is wonderful, Don."

"Sure is."

"I'm awfully glad you asked me along."

"You're sweating like a draught horse."

"I'm in good shape but this forest works you hard. I've never seen so much autumn olive and late blackberries in one place. I'm not surprised there's birds in here."

Robb's a fit and sturdy man of fifty. He's competing in the big Ice Man Cometh trail bike race from Kalkaska to Traverse City in early November and trains like a mad man all year round. He's also the publisher of Edible WOW, the down state magazine about organic and local farming.

"How does Derek move through these woods so fast? I can't keep up," he asked.

"It's a mystery."

"That last stand of poplar was so thick I had to turn back. There's not five inches between the saplings and they snap back at you like vicious little whips."

"I know. That's why I stick to the open trail."

"It seems to me Derek walks through trees like nothing's there."
A single sudden blast of Derek's 20 gauge bent the air around us.

As we talked, the sun came out and lit the woods as though someone flipped a switch. Down the slope towards the pond we could just make out Harley popping up and down through tall dying ferns to get his bearings as he sniffed for the warm body of a grouse. We could just make out Derek's orders but we couldn't see him.

"Get the bird, Harley. Find the bird."

Quitting While You're Ahead
Friday, October 30th, 2009

I woke up last Thursday around 4:00 AM and heard our newly winterized cottage on the west shore of Mullett Lake groan in ways I'd never heard before. The east wind was throwing itself at my new vinyl siding like Greeks punishing the walls of Troy. It made so much noise I grabbed the new flashlight Sal bought last week and stepped out into the weather with my parka thrown over my pajamas. I pointed the beam out into the night towards the hordes of waves attacking my property. High heavy white caps advanced one by one in a stinging rain and pounded our Lake Superior rocks built as a breakwater. I hurried back to safety and up to bed but didn't sleep.

On Friday the wind got even stronger during the day. Before I left for work, I walked by the windows facing the storm with a book of matches, lighting one every few steps to gauge the draft. With 40 mph gusts howling around us, what I thought was pretty air tight was not. I could barely keep a flame going when I held it close to the glass. The winds continued all day and didn't slow until well after dark.

In the morning it was bitter and dreary with spits of rain from every passing cloud. But the big breeze was coming from the west.

The house was silent again. As we waited in the warmth of our bathrobes for the coffee machine to beep, Sally reminded me about the promise we'd made to each other the night before while the lake was acting like an angry child. She knew the sounds of our cottage in the storm had my finger on the worry trigger.

"We're going to have some fun today," she said as she poured a cup for both of us. "We're going on an adventure."

To us that meant spontaneous thinking and doing something we'd never done before. It had been a long time since we last gave it a try.

"Right. To heck with the weather."

At noon, without any planning, we sat down at the bar at The Key Hole in Mackinaw City and ordered perch sandwiches.

"Now what, Sal?"

"Haven't a clue."

"Your call today."

"How about I take you on a tour of St. Ignace?"

She'd been over the bridge the day before the storm hit. Her contact for her new teaching job with North Central Michigan College had showed her around town. If enough people signed up for classes, she'd be teaching English in the Upper Peninsula starting in January.

Across the Straits, as we paid our bridge toll, she came up with another idea.

"You'll get to know St. Ignace some other day. Let's try our luck at the casino."

"O.K." Gambling was the last thing I thought she'd want to do. I guess that made it perfect. "What's our limit? How much do we risk?"

"How much do we have in cash?"

"About eighty bucks.

"Eighty bucks it is. Forty each. We stick together."

Twenty minutes later we entered the lobby at Kewadin. People were glued to what we presumed were their lucky machines so we found two slots with graphics Sal liked and plopped down. One was called AquaLand and the other something about Lucky Sevens. We each slipped a virgin five spot into the openings that suck them in. Around and around the tumblers went. We pressed the "bet it all" button and pulled the hand levers that give the "one armed bandits" their moniker. After repeating our hopeful naiveté for five minute we didn't have much left. A couple of winners, mostly losers. The pattern all casinos count on.

We laughed each time we lost. We patted each other on the back for our luck when it slipped through the barricade of house odds. There was clanging and flashing all around us. The regulars seemed to win more than they were losing.

As we crossed the Mackinac Bridge on our way home, Sal opened the windows to blasts of cold air just for the hell of it. We'd won exactly nine dollars over three hours, enough to cover the cost of crossing over on a whim with plenty to spare for the half gallon of milk we needed for cereal.

Sitting in front of a raging fire in the hearth, Sally and I told silly boastful stories about knowing when to quit while you're ahead.

We slept through the night like hibernating bears.

Night of the Beaver Moon
Friday, November 6th, 2009

With an armful of wood last night I looked up into the cold windless sky at the Beaver Moon. That's what most astronomers in the Northern Hemisphere call the full moon of early November. The upper ridges of soft slow-moving cumulus clouds gathered the silver light, happy with their appearance for the first time in weeks. The trees in my yard, stripped bare of their stubborn brown leaves by days of wicked winds, stood still, mesmerized by their own shadows.

Our month long tussle with dark grey hours and evening downpours was over for a while.

Back inside our Mullett Lake cottage, I stacked my load in our wood box and placed a heavy, dry unsplit piece of maple into the new woodburner. I locked down the side door and opened the flue for full throttle flames.

"Should we take a walk?" I asked Sally who was curled up on the couch reading her third book in four days.

"Now?"

"Why not? You wouldn't believe how bright it is. Too bad the kids didn't have this kind of moonlight for trick-or-treating."

"Sure. Let's go."

A few minutes later we stepped out onto the North Central State Trail in our coats, scarves and hats and started south. It didn't take me long to fill the delightful silence with the sound of my own voice.

"According to the Farmers' Almanac the name Beaver Moon comes from the reference by native tribes who told the Europeans this moon meant it was time for trapping beaver in earnest. " I said as Sal shuffled along beside me. "Plenty of beaver pelts meant survival in the months ahead. Some refer to it as the Full Frosty Moon but that sounds more like a chocolate milk shake."

"Can we just walk along without the anthropology lessons?"

I barely heard her as I kept yapping. Her only defense was a sharp change of subject.

"Are you going to buy that used generator?"

"No."

"No?"

"No. I'm done. I've had it with my chronic get ready for winter overload. Time to turn the page."

I'd received advice from a critical source over the weekend about doing the generator thing or not.

The words had lodged between my ears came from my old dad in Minnesota. Pop's got a thousand health issues keeping him from

47

speaking his mind. Post-polio Parkinson's is the big one. Mom works with it every day. His mind is clear though, sharp as a razor blade. His words are usually impossible to understand when he slumps way right in his motorized wheelchair.

A few weeks ago we got him a Skype camera for his PC, a device that makes your computer a darn good picture phone. It was a simple birthday present to keep in touch since we couldn't make it to Duluth recently for his 90th celebration.

Last Friday night, when my folks appeared on the monitor, we caught up on things: my new job and Sally's pending work at the college in St. Ignace and their latest dinner out with their old cadre of aging pals.

Mom leaned close and smiled into the camera, fascinated at seeing us so clearly. In the background Sal and I could see my dad pecking away at his new Stephen Hawking device that lets him speak in full sentences. He clicked a final button and the machine spit out the words he'd been working so hard on.

"You will electrocute yourself. Let power company fix lines." His voice sounded exactly like the robot on "Lost in Space."

I told him I knew about pulling the main breaker before firing up a generator when the power goes out. We waited a few minutes for his forefinger to type a reply.

"Danger is when power comes back on."

When Sal and I made it back to the cottage from a long walk communing with the Beaver Moon, we each grabbed a log and gently placed them into the new stove. We stood there for a while warming our hands.

"I hope it snows this week," she said as she leaned against me. "It's time."

It Will Be Okay
Friday, November 20th, 2009

A couple of weekends ago I drove down to Columbus from Mullet Lake in Sal's Camry. I made the trip because I needed to see my son Max. He'd asked for some time with me. For two years he's been producing music and doing the books at the recording studio in Ohio, the one we built before the economic meltdown arrived.

"Here's a jar of applesauce for him," Sal said as we short-hugged in the cold morning darkness that hung over our gravel driveway.

I took the Ball Jar from her and sat in the driver's seat, putting my seat cushion into place underneath me. She was doing the talking for a change.

"I'd like to say I want to go with you but that would be a lie."

"I know."

"The forecast is fabulous for the weekend. I'm going take long walks and ride my bike a lot."

Our Michigan autumn has provided little encouragement to our experiment of living far north. Record cold for October. Nearly record rain. The drab and droopy cedars around our gravel parking area seemed to know a few nice days were approaching. I imagined they were saying bon voyage, and just like Sal, happy at the prospect of a peaceful few days of sun.

"You've been waiting for nice fall days for a long time."

I suddenly felt like I shouldn't go at all; maybe handle everything with a thorough phone call.

"Be careful. Watch for deer. Call me when you get there." She leaned inside the door fame and kissed me on the cheek. "Don't worry. Max is a grown man and he only wants your advice."

In my rearview mirror I hoped to see her waving a bold goodbye but saw her pick up our little Jack Russell terrier instead and start back to the cottage.

On I-75 my grey matter left me alone and my senses started asserting themselves. The sun squeaked under a thin strip of clouds on the eastern horizon as I neared the Indian River Exit. Warm yellow rays flooded the highway when the nose of the car passed Wolverine. Near Vanderbilt the persistent fog turned soft and orange and gave up its efforts to keep the night alive. I opened the window slightly and the smell of drying leaves filled the car. It was Indian Summer.

The eight hour journey was instantaneous, the hours minutes. It was almost 70F when I turned onto the uneasy familiarity of the outer belt at the edge of the big city. My peaceful and empty mind flashed back to its oldest habits. I started to think about things I couldn't do anything about.

As I chugged along towards downtown, a thousand expensive European cars blurred by, rabbits passing an aimless turtle. I was able, however, to kick my trepidations into the back seat and it seemed to work as I pulled in front of Max's apartment building.

When I knocked on his front door, I saw him through the glass. He popped up and rushed to greet me. We embraced for a millisecond. I hadn't seen him since he came up to Cheboygan in the middle of the summer. He'd gained some weight since then. His jet black hair matched his growing beard. In a second we were in the Camry and on our way to the Blue Danube restaurant just north of the OSU campus.

We compared dreams of an uncertain future, wolfing down hot beef sandwiches and watching the football game as we talked.

"I really want to go to graduate school at New York University," he told me. "It's a perfect program for me. I'm working on the application and the financial aid. I've got my portfolio almost ready. And I need to leave home like you and Mom."

"Wow."

We finished our dinners, paid the bill, and slid out the door past fans in Scarlet and Grey happy the Buckeyes were demolishing the

Nittany Lions.

As we neared Sal's car we saw the lights were on. We got inside. The sun visor on his side was down. The glove compartment hung open, violated. My briefcase was gone, my laptop too. My ten year old address book was missing from the dashboard. It felt like my very soul had been clipped.

Max looked at me with a deep, burning sadness. I don't remember much of the next hour. I think I just followed him around while he searched in dumpsters along the alleyways nearby. We drove back to his place, sat on his couch close together and filled out an online police report.

"Dad. Are you going to be all right?"

"I don't think I can take this, Max." I rested my head on his shoulder for what seemed like another month of cold rains.

"It'll be okay, Dad."

Driving home to the Straits on Sunday morning, somewhere around West Branch, it dawned on me. Max had come to my rescue. He'd done the comforting a parent usually does. Max had been the one who was calm and steadfast in the storm, a sailor ready for life on the sea.

I turned on the music for the first time since leaving Columbus and cranked up my favorite songs for the rest of the ride back to Mullett Lake.

My Browning Twenty Gauge Shotgun
Friday, November 27th, 2009

To me there's always been something deeply symbolic and beautiful about my twenty gauge 1963 Belgian made Browning over-and-under shotgun. My dad bought it for me the same year it was made. It's light, perfectly balanced, and as comfortable in your left hand as your right. The perfect grouse hunting weapon. My old man had heard they were going to shift manufacturing to Japan in a couple of years and the news didn't make him happy.

Actually, the gun I have now is not the gun he gave when I was ten years old. That one was lost in a fire in Iowa City a few days after Sal tentatively said yes to my proposal of marriage by not saying anything at all. That, of course, is another story.

My dad looked around for ten years for the exact same gun and handed me the replacement with little ceremony on his way to Florida a long time ago. I knew he spent a fortune on it. In the early 1990's they were going for twenty times their purchase price. I didn't have any idea where to hunt in Ohio and, as I remember it, barely thanked him for the gift.

In early November I took the shotgun to Keith's Hunting and Fishing Store on Main Street in Cheboygan where their gunsmith spent almost thirty hours working on it. The mechanism was so gummed up, he said, that it was a good thing I was taking care of it, that it was more dangerous to me than to the grouse I hunted.

I knew only one barrel would shoot. The trigger took a Sampson finger to pull hard enough to fire the gun. I'd been sending lead off at odd angles in the forest all fall, missing nearly every bird. It was Saturday afternoon, just a few hours of daylight before the start of rifle deer season in northern Michigan, the last day for walking through the woods after partridge until after Thanksgiving.

"That'll be $67."

"Are you sure? That doesn't sound right. Be fair to yourself, Earl."

He dismissed my concern with a wave as he walked around the fifty-year-old scratched glass display counter to ring me up.

"Only had a small pile of guns and scopes that came in a couple of weeks ago. Not as much work as there used to be. I was just tinkering with the Browning." He explained how the recoil impact against my shoulder resets a tightly wound spring and readies the second barrel for a quick shot. "It was so mucked up with grime that even after I cleaned it out pretty good, nothing. I thought the thing was permanently all wound up. Scared me when it released. Back-fired the damn mechanism through the room like a missile."

"Gee."

"Store the gun barrel-down. That way the bluing won't run down and get into your firing pins and everything else."

I paid the bill, drove around the lake to my favorite place off Hackleburg Road, and didn't see a bird. Back at my car, I slipped the Browning into its case and slid it onto the backseat. Some men drove by with a load of stuff for making deer camp, a four wheeler in the back of their pickup looking anxious to get on with the hunt like the rest of the troupe. They tipped their fluorescent caps to me. God, they looked happy.

Back at the cottage on Mullett Lake, Sally and I spent the night at opposite ends of the first floor. She read and watched a favorite show. I sat at the dining room table with the wood stove roaring a few feet away.

I studied my surroundings as though I'd been plucked from my past in Minnesota, lifted from almost thirty years in Ohio and dropped softly into the future. Pinewood plank walls glowed yellow gold. My shadow and those from our straight backed chairs danced all around me. I looked outside through the picture window towards the still and open big lake water. Crystal sharp stars shined brilliant through the barren maple hanging out over the shoreline. A thousand tiny holiday lights shimmered along the arms of the old tree.

Finally it was time for bed. Sal asked me what I was doing with the Browning across my lap.

"I don't know. Smelling it I guess. I'm thinking about my dad. And my brother and sisters, too."

She walked up the stairs one firm step at a time, scuffing her slippers on the carpeted steps in emphatic harmony to the words she left hanging in the dry warm air.

It felt like she was leaving me alone because I needed time with the gun without anyone else around. The Browning was an old best family friend I hadn't seen in years who dropped by suddenly and needed a place on the couch. We needed to drink shots of whiskey together. We needed to talk for a while about hunting and family secrets and Thanksgivings past before it was time to sleep.

Forgot the Snow Shovel
Friday, December 4th, 2009

At work the other day, my co-worker Mary asked if I was ready for winter.

"Got the snow blower all set and your shovel by the door?"

After all my machinations and constant chatter about Sal and my efforts to get our summer place on Mullett Lake ready for our first winter up north, the question didn't surprise me. My answer did.

"God. I don't think I have a shovel. I can't believe it. I don't have a snow shovel. Gave it to the people who bought our house down in Ohio. How could I forget something like that?"

"That's Okay. You'll pay a little more for it, though, now that the snow is coming."

"I just can't believe it. I forgot the shovel."

"They say it's gonna snow tonight. Not much. Maybe an inch or something. It's still pretty warm."

It was after 5:00 P.M. downtown and it was time to close down the office. She locked the front door facing Main Street, signaling the end of the day though I had a few things to finish up at my computer station. I stayed behind as most of the team started for home.

An hour later I found myself driving south along the Straits Highway away from Lake Huron and the City of Cheboygan through the first real snowflakes since April. The windshield wipers came on by themselves. Or did they? I was listening to an old country western classic on the radio and daydreaming in the dark behind my high beams. I was thinking about too many things and nothing at all. I was peering into the falling white blanket of winter's first night.

When I splashed my front tires through the snow rimmed puddles along Silver Beach Road by the lake shore, I saw the lights of our place shining through the resilient cedars at the edge of our property. The barren maples in our yard seemed to reach out to my headlights as I parked in the gravel turnaround. Like every time I'd come home since Labor Day, I wished for a garage for my car, a place for the old girl to hide from Arctic Blasts and Giant Drifts. I figured those unforgiving twins were waiting in northern Manitoba for just the right opportunity to move hand in hand across the Great Lakes into our little Straits neighborhood.

Inside the cottage, the fire was hot in the woodburner. Sal had Christmas lights strung along the mantle, around the picture windows, and up the stairs. Garlands of holly branches and pine boughs followed our twinkling holiday lights through every downstairs room.

Maizie, our sprite little 12 year old Jack Russell Terrier, jumped up on the couch to greet me, proud of the decorations.

"Gee. It looks absolutely beautiful in here."

"Thanks," Sal said with a grin.

"I mean you've really transformed this place. It reminds me of home."

"It is home."

"It is. I know."

"We need to get a tree now."

"Isn't a little early? It'll dry out by Christmas."

"We need a tree. My decision."

"Okay. We need a tree."

"How was work?" she said as she got up from her favorite chair. I followed her into the kitchen where she threw ice into a tall glass for me.

"Good."

"How?"

"I don't know. Just good." How'd your writing go today?"

"Wonderful. I love the new scenes."

Out the kitchen window, what had been a faint but steady snowfall was now clumps of wet flakes stuck together. They were as big as fifty cent coins and it seemed they were just as heavy. In the minute we stood there looking out, a half an inch of white stuff covered the soft green and brown grasses of our yard, tucking the ground into bed for a good four month sleep.

"Don't have a snow shovel, Sal."

"That's weird."

"I know. Hard to believe I could forget that. I'll get one tomorrow."

I made five trips to the woodpile while Sal ground black pepper and threw more vegetables into a steaming pot on the stove.

We ate turkey soup at the dining room table and looked out over the open water. We went for a walk and threw a few mushy snowballs at each other. Maizie raced through the empty white yards of our neighbors like she had the scent of a rabbit. But it was the snow she was after, the feel of it between her toes as she streaked into the darkness, running endlessly around and around her favorite giant trees.

The Things All Around Me
Friday, December 11th, 2009

Why was I suddenly taking notice of things like I've been blind all my life?

The sky so blue and deep it looked like a painting by Michelangelo. Three Canada geese with an inch of snow on their backs swimming past the rocks where my dock was three months ago. The surface of Mullett Lake resisting a solid freeze by conjuring a wind where there was none. The angles of fallen timber in the woods. The length of icicles hanging along the gutters and their odd individual shapes. Silver light from the waning Long Night Moon sliding past the curtains of our bedroom at night. The pure whiteness of lake effect snow.

Was it me recognizing my world in Technicolor detail or some stranger who snuck into my body and then my clothes?

Whoever it was, he wore my exact same size and knew precisely where everything was. Right down to my stash of fresh long underwear and new heavy cotton socks. Including my secret pack of cigarettes and my hidden box of Diamond Strike-On-The-Box matches.

Sal could tell I was in dreamland when she came down for coffee.

"What's up?" she asked as she floated past me across the linoleum squares of our kitchen floor.

"Have no idea," I lied as she poured a cup.

"No idea?"

"I'm seeing things I never noticed before. I'm seeing everything."

"Everything?"

"I know. It sounds kind of weird."

"No, it sounds right."

She hustled up the stairway to gain higher ground from my open-eyed stare out onto the lake. Yellow red sunlight burst from a ten inch slat below the heavy clouds on the eastern horizon. Gold filled the room. Amber resins seemed to flow from our knotted pine walls.

A load of wood appeared in my arms by magic. When I stoked the woodburner, a blast of hot air whooshed past my ears. My tongue was sour and sweet at the same time. I pushed the last piece of hardwood into the stove and stepped back. The stove pipe squawked and creaked as it inhaled.

Computer, Man. Go to your computer. You brought home some

work from the office. Get going. Check your email. Get started.

Wherever the voice of reason came from, I listened.

The emails were routine. The National Weather Service website was not.

A meteorologist guy from Kansas was calling a serious low pressure system heading our way in the middle of the week... "the Perfect Storm of December approaching the Great Lakes."

God. Did he have to say "Perfect Storm?" I saw the movie.

"Blizzard conditions will prevail in northern Michigan with sustained winds of 50 to 60 miles and hour in some places along Lake Huron."

I stood up and walked to the picture window. The still unfrozen waters of Mullett Lake looked calm enough. But purple grey clouds were elbowing their way over the opposite shore and whispering a warning. They said something like "...good luck getting outta here once my friends show up."

The weatherman was right. Something really big was on the way.

Later in the morning on my way to work I stopped at the used car lot where a 2000 Jeep still sat facing the Straits Highway like it had been for the last six months. Within twenty minutes the deal was done. My old front wheel drive Swedish station wagon horse traded for a solid little Willy's. 180,000 miles exchanged for 160,000. The four wheel drive was mine. After work I drove home through the gathering winds of early winter rather proud of myself.

What could go wrong now? I had the Jeep.

I was confident about things at dinner. Sal told me what she'd heard about the snowfall. We expected eight to ten inches. Before bedtime I laid-in a quarter cord of wood, filling half the kitchen in maple and birch.

At 4:00 a.m. the house exploded with piercing whistles and the clanging of loose weather stripping in a hurricane. My feet hit the carpet in an instant. My dream of Sally and me in our old house in

Ohio with our little boys pulling presents from under the tree on Christmas morning disappeared on the pillow.

From the upstairs hallway I could hear giant waves whacking the shore as an outdoor wind rushed through my flannel pajamas. Half way down the steps I saw our French door leading to the lake wide open. The storm was perfect all right, perfectly aligned from the east, laughing at the feeble attempt by my new insulated storm door to keep it from muscling its way in.

I pushed the door back in place, jammed the bolt locks back down, and rolled up our wool couch blanket for insulation along the floor where a jet stream of cold air powered into the room.

With more wood in the heater, I pulled a straight backed chair from the kitchen and sat down to keep warm. Sounds I'd never heard before raced around my cottage like children screaming with glee at a birthday party. I sat there listening to the things all around me until first light.

Every Day is Garbage Day
Friday, December 18th, 2009

My father-in-law told me something a few years back I've never forgotten.

'When you get to be my age, every day is garbage day. You take it to the street one day; you wake up the next and it's time to do it again.

That's what it's like when you get older. That's how fast time passes when you've only got a good handful of grains left in the hour glass.'

That's what I was thinking about in the grey cold early morning. I dragged our hard packed can of garbage through the falling flakes along the crystal white path I'd just cut to Silver Beach Road with the snowblower. A minute later I started the Jeep and drove out our winding little road away from Mullett Lake to the Straits Highway.

Fifteen straight mornings of lake effect snow so far. Regular as garbage day. I could barely see a thing through the windshield.

The Jeep whined and wheezed as I accelerated. What was that smell? Bacon grease? Why was my new ride making breakfast for itself under the hood? The wheel wobble in my palms sent nerves of worry down my spine. My tongue felt like someone threw dirt in my mouth. I'd bought a lemon.

I pulled into Village Auto Repair just a quarter mile north of our cottage. I'd always taken my new but very used cars to a shop for diagnostics after the purchase. This was my first one up north. I'd scheduled an appointment with Fred the day before.

I knocked on the side door and stepped inside the cinder block fortress, kicking my feet together to remove the slush from my boots. A big Olds 98 looked embarrassed high in the air on the lift in one bay, a pile of mud and brown grasses under the grill on the cement floor. Fred didn't move from his desk chair in the corner but waved me over. Hot air threw itself at my face from a giant furnace blower near the ceiling. He was typing the work order for my Jeep into his laptop.

He extended a gnarly hand to me. A smile escaped from the corner of his mouth. His grip was a vice. He spoke slowly, making sure he had everything listed from our previous conversation.

"Oil change, check the brakes, new transmission oil and filter, chassis lube." he said. "You want us to make sure she's good for the winter."

Fred's words slid into the shop air and mixed with the roar of the heater fan, each syllable waiting patiently for the next.

"Yup. I do. There's a shimmy in the front end, too. I smell something funny when I step on the gas. And it doesn't like to respond without some pretty odd noises."

Fred's chief mechanic, Jamie, pulled more debris from under the bumper of the car on the hoist. Wet muck flopped onto his shoes. He joined us and we shook hands.

"We'll figure it out." Jamie exclaimed.

"What happened to that one?" I asked, pointing at the Oldsmobile.

"Lady ran into a ditch. Didn't do much damage though. Just missed a guide wire and a pole," Fred said with respect for the driver's good luck.

Fred told me to follow him so I could take a look at his heating unit behind the building. It was massive as a locomotive. Hungry for fuel. It belched smoke when he opened it. The logs stacked around it were big like the biceps of Atlas. No one man would could ever throw one of these pieces of timber into the screaming heat by himself.

"I gotta go, Fred. This is amazing. I want one."

Before I'd left a half hour before, Sal had told me the walk home along the North Central Michigan Trail along the lake shore would be good for my circulation.

I pushed my 1969 Sorel boots into two inches of fresh white fluff near the abandoned one room station building right by the lake and headed south on the trail towards home. A charcoal sky descended on me as the snow closed ranks.

The lake was still open, constantly moving to keep the inevitable from overcoming it. Down the pathway, the longest straight stretch between Cheboygan and Gaylord, the lights of a distant snowmobile shook like a train light in the night as though the North Central Michigan Railroad was back in business. My feet were cold. The wings of twenty or so mallards warped the air above me. They splashed into the bay, happy to find open water.

Back in our kitchen I poured the last cup of hot coffee into my mug.

Two hours later Fred called.

"I'm coming down to get you. We're done."

"Already?"

"Sure are. You've got a pretty good automobile here."

"You mean it? I got a good one?"
"You got a good one."

Coyote Christmas
Thursday, December 24th, 2009

Sally is down in Ohio for Christmas week with our two grown sons and her Dad. It'll be pretty much our dog Maizie and I until she brings Max and Hart up to Northern Michigan the day after the big day. Our own little holiday is coming. I imagine mostly new underwear, socks, popcorn, and gag gifts. We'll have the two of them under our roof again, hostage for three whole days. I can hardly wait.

The day she left I was on my way to the laundry room in the back cabin when I heard the tinkling slushy sound of remnant ice in the waves. For the last week the waters of Mullett Lake began the early morning with high hopes of resting for four consecutive months. But right through the first days of astronomical winter, humane temperatures and steady winds drowned the shiny new surface before it was truly born. It reappeared at night in shattered crystals along our rocky shore.

As I stood in the late afternoon light, hypnotized by the music of icicles in surf, I realized I wasn't alone in our yard.

The first coyote I'd ever seen around our place tiptoed towards the cedars along the border of neighbor John's property thirty yards away. The animal's wild canine ears stood erect. He tucked a thick bushy tail between his hind legs.

The confident little animal stopped in slow motion and twisted his body around without lifting his paws from the crusty snow. He looked me square in the face. There was still plenty of light to see his whiskers and the steam of his breath.

His famished tongue disappeared into his mouth as he sniffed the air. His fur was long and thick, creamy white down his throat, yellowish grey down his back, and it waved in the wind like winter wheat.

I stepped forward one stride but he didn't budge, another and he jumped forward like I'd stuck him with a broom on the rear end. He returned my glare with even more curiosity. The golden ring inside his brown eyes glowed through the descending night.

Maizie barked a high pitched plea for me to return to the warmth of the cottage.

In an instant I thought about how she struggled in eight inches of new wet snow on the ground, how she wasn't a third the size of her carnivorous canine cousin. She was a Jack Russell. Bred in Australia for protecting outback ranches. Maybe the coyote had been hanging around all week watching her and waiting. Maybe the coyote was looking for Christmas dinner.

I waved my arms and slapped my gloves together. The coyote took one baby step towards cover. I picked up the snow shovel by the front door and stepped over the bank past the artesian well and another ten steps closer to him. He held his ground.

"You're supposed to be afraid of humans!" I yelled. My words flew over my shoulder with a gust from the south. "Haven't you heard?"

The coyote stopped retreating like he'd been insulted, as though he didn't want anyone telling him how to feel. He began a sleek crouch straight towards me like I couldn't see him.

"Get the heck outta here you little mongrel!"

He inched closer.

I lifted the shovel over my head and waited for his attack, his all out spring at my throat. I knew it was coming.

My night shirt was damp from sweat when I bolted upright in my bed. The coyote's reconnaissance of our land had been a dream. A very clear one, but still a dream. My sheets and down comforter were indistinguishable, pretzeled together over my chest. I pulled the mess to the floor and put on my slippers and bathrobe and went downstairs at 3:00 a.m. with Maizie right behind me.

I threw her favorite toy, a squeaking rubber monster called Goofy Guy, around the room like there was no tomorrow. Christmas lights dangled from pine boughs around the windows and up the stairs. I got on the floor on my knees and spun her around on the faded Persian rug. She jumped up and over me and around me and under the couch and over the couch and through my side room office and around the dining room table and into the kitchen and back again.

When I reached for her, she squealed. She sprinted a circle to the back of our Christmas tree and plopped down and wouldn't come out. Our little electric train came down the track and she knocked over the locomotive with the toy engineer at the controls. She did it on purpose.

I retrieved a fake sirloin treat from the cupboard. Maizie wolfed it down as though she'd earned it as a prize at the county fair.

She didn't notice when I moved my Browning 20 gauge shotgun to the front hall closet and hid four shells along the edge of the rafter beams. This would be a different kind of Christmas.

Charades Anyone?
Thursday, December 31st, 2009

Last Sunday afternoon Sal and I took our sons Max and Hart on a little tour of the Straits. We crossed the Mackinac Bridge through a sinking grey snowfall in my little Jeep to show them what winter looked like in the Upper Peninsula. We picked the Kewadin Casino in St. Ignace as a destination because neither Max nor Hart had ever been inside one. We had no real money for gambling. It was a drive for no good reason other than our joy at being together up north for the first time in half a decade. We each lost twenty bucks pretty fast. We took pictures. We headed for home.

As we approached the cottage on Mullett Lake at 5:40 P.M. we could see our lights welcoming us home through the barren aspens and sapling maples. Then suddenly all was dark. It was like somebody was hiding inside our place, saw us smiling our way down the road through five inches of fresh snow and decided to play a little trick on us. Maybe it was our dog Maizie, we thought, but that was impossible. She's a little Jack Russell terrier who's afraid of the dark.

Inside the blackness of our house we stomped our boots and lit every candle. We loaded fresh batteries in all three flashlights. Max and Hart trudged behind me to the woodpile for five or six loads of hardwood. We stuffed the main fireplace and the wood stove, started two roaring blazes, and waited. And waited.

Sal could see my instinct for over-the-top worrying kick in.

"Relax. There's nothing we can do about it."

On the phone, the power company refused to predict a restoration time so we called Breakers Bar and Grille down the Straits Highway in Topinabee and they had electricity. Derek told us the whole city of Cheboygan was out of power and that he'd hold a table for us.

Just past Long Point, Sally pointed at the Moon above the windshield wipers.

"Wow. Look at that."

"That's the Wolf Moon," I said.

"What?" asked Max.

"Please. Don't ask him to elaborate." Sal knew my passion for spewing myriad little facts like bullets from a machine gun and tried to plug my barrel before I got going. She was too late.

"The names of the full moons in North America come from the Algonquin language. European settlers pretty much embraced the terms. Wolves began their night-long howls of hunger around the New Year."

"Got it, Dad," piped Hart from the back seat.

At our table near the bar, we ate hamburgers as though we

hadn't seen food in days. I poked the redial button on my mobile between bites, harassing the automated customer service system at Consumers Energy.

People poured through the door at Breakers. Adventurers dressed in snowmobile suits. Couples in cashmere. Folks in jeans and long sleeve t-shirts, regulars and strangers. Holiday weekenders with their kids. Grandparents and great-grandparents. Babies. In a power outage on a Sunday night, with plenty of light and warmth on the menu, you've got the best restaurant on the planet.

Back home we settled in around the hearth as the largest fire ever built rose up and threw great waves of gold light between the rafter beams. The blaze danced higher and higher up the chimney. The sweet smell of ozone filled the room as the fire cracked and boasted its heat. We stared at the candles flickering towards the draft of the fireplace as the dog moved closer for warmth.

My thoughts drifted to the water in our pipes that wasn't moving, to the prediction of 5 degrees Fahrenheit for a low by 5:00 A.M.

As the room warmed we discarded our wool blankets. I had a vision from my past as a boy at our summer cabin in Minnesota. I saw my brother and my sisters and my mom watch my dad make his own kind of rescue fire to brighten the dark night when the power went out. My dad didn't mess around when he wanted a good fire. He was a kerosene man.

I thought about the game we played while my dad sat in his chair and admired his handiwork.

"Charades anyone?"

My gang cringed as I declared the start of the game. I jumped to my feet, my backside to the roaring furnace. Around my right earlobe I mimicked the turn of a reel of film. Movie. I held up two fingers. Two word movie. I touched my forefinger to my wrist. First word. I mimed slipping a ring on my imaginary bride's finger, kissing her long on the lips, and walking back down the aisle with her on my arm.

"Wedding Crashers," yelled Hart. Maizie sat up, confused.

Max declared he wouldn't do any titles but he'd be a good audience and try to guess. Sal and Hart the same. I kept going.

The more ridiculous my contortions, the greater the belly laughs. An hour later I was exhausted and plopped on the couch next to Hart. The utility guys six miles away at the main Cheboygan substation threw a switch. Our Christmas tree lights appeared like magic. The string of twinkling stars along the mantle seemed happy as we to have juice back in the outlets. Our little train engine at the base of the tree awakened with electricity and chugged around like nothing in the world could bother it again.

Let's Keep Going
Saturday, January 9th, 2010

A light snow covered the cars in our gravel driveway. It blanketed the garbage cans, the woodpiles, the back cabin, the well gazebo, the front deck, and most of all, our memories of the last two weeks along the shores of Mullett Lake.

For that, Sal and I were grateful. The previous handful of brilliant December days had been filled with the visage of our sons who were finally with us again, twinkling Christmas lights on the tree, ham and turkey with gravy and corn pudding, rich sauces of summer fruit, golden sunsets, a towering silver moon, a power outage, the trip to the casino in St. Ignace, caramel and chocolates and toffee on my tongue, our dog's whining sorrow as the boys left to return to their lives in New York and Columbus, the arrival of lake friends up for the New Year's carnival, and dignified long-necked swans cruising the few open spaces left across the theater of white and grey out the window.

The new year had arrived, and we both felt ready for it though unsure about its steady growth into true winter.

The Cheboygan Daily Tribune Columns

It was a late Monday afternoon, just before a purple twisted cloud of ice crystals disappeared over the eastern horizon across the lake. On the radio in my home office a hopeful waltz of bagpipes rose into the knotted pine ceiling of our cottage. A tiny fire Sal lit earlier in the day still glowed in the great stone fireplace. I put three dry logs of hardwood onto the coals and it jumped to life before my eyes.

She put her fingers to her lips with reproach for any suggestion of things I wanted to say. She held up her cross country ski boots, the black ones I got her for Christmas along with pairs of almost never used skis and poles.

I bought them from Doug, a beautiful man of 77 years with shoulder length grey hair who could not use his them anymore because his back was hot with pain. Doug and his wife purchased their skis a couple of years before with the promise of forever traversing the trails of their ancestors. We talked. They offered tea. I bought the equipment for a song.

With some trouble, Sal and I managed to get our toe pins into the bindings and began our journey into the darkening night towards Long Point. Our dog Maizie perched on a chair and looked out at us through the living room window. She usually barked rabidly for us to let her come along but not this time.

The waning moon disappeared. The snow that retreated earlier in the day fell again in earnest as the lake sang in odd cracking harmonies, turning into a solid sheet of ice for the first time.

We veered towards the untracked new snow between the yards of our summer neighbors. We wouldn't see them for months. Not a word was said as we started to find a fluid rhythm in the tracks we carved into the white powder. My hands began to numb. My nose the same. Sally too. We skied under great barren maples, between cedars, through fence breaks and hedges now forgotten as demarcation of ownership. We poled, slid and skated around birdfeeders and poles of electric lights at rest for the remainder of northern Michigan's January, February, March....

My dream of the coyote in my yard two weeks before slipped between my eyes, his soft threatening breath as real as the arctic air. I thought about the uneasy flocks of mallards and goldeneyes that covered the open stretches of the lake all weekend knowing that rock hard ice was coming. A bald eagle stood on the ice for hours watching them. Had he been fishing for a last great meal from the lake or was he just waiting for inexperienced ducks trapped in the floes?

I lagged a few feet behind Sally. My lungs gasped for more air. My thighs ached. My hips joints throbbed.

We stopped in our tracks when we smelled the peaty aroma of a wood fire. We could taste the smoke coming from our hearth a half mile behind us.

"C'mon. Let's keep going," she said.

Skating on Thin Ice
Saturday, January 16th, 2010

Last weekend Sal and I planned a strictly budgeted, fun couple of days: a Saturday trip for $9 in gas to Charlevoix where we'd never been before and the next day Don and Sal's Winterfest Extravaganza Competition. We'd be the only contestants.

Saturday was bitter cold but brighter than any day in a long time. South along Mullett from our cottage, we noticed a few people ice fishing out on the lake. As we passed Crooked Lake in Conway, a festival of folks in snowmobile suits crowded together out on the ice attending their fishing lines and staring into their newly augured holes. Crooked Lake had been safe for almost a month.

On the drive through Hemingway's town and along Lake Michigan's coast to Charlevoix harbor, great sheets of pack ice floated in the blue water waiting for the right wind to pile on shore. In downtown, ducks swam in a circle near an empty pier like miniature Coast

Guard cutters keeping a small opening free from ice.

We ate a surprisingly cheap and exquisite lunch at Whitney's Oyster Bar and stopped at Oleson's in Petoskey on the way back for a fresh loaf of French bread. We wore sunglasses. Ah... sunglasses.

As we neared home we planned Sunday's winter sports program.

For the last three days the clear shining surface between Dodge Point and our place screamed at me, yelling 'come, skate,' and I whispered in agreement each time. I used to play pond hockey growing up in Duluth and remembered glorious days at our family's lake cabin cruising across the ice before the snow arrived. Speed skating would be the first event of our private little Olympiad.

"I'll skate to Harry's and back," I offered. "You take a couple of photos. It'll be great." Before we left for Charlevoix, three snowmobiles had raced across the frozen lake near shore. It made me feel confident about the strength of the ice. "Then we hold the cross country skiing event. Just two miles. You know I'm out of shape. Then a little snowshoeing. We'll take photos of everything and email them to my dad."

"Can the first event be bringing breakfast in bed to your spouse?" Sal countered. "And you're the only contestant?"

"Sure."

"No pictures please."

Sunday morning a blinding yellow reflection of the rising sun threw itself through the curtainless windows of our upstairs bedroom. Nonetheless I slept in and flunked the opening ceremonies.

After I stretched my hamstrings for a half hour, Sal followed me outside. We crept down the embankment of great round boulders to Mullett Lake 40 feet out our back door. My skates hung by their laces around my neck. I was anxious to get started.

"Are you sure it's safe?" she asked.

"There's nothing to worry about," I replied. "The snowmobiles were out here yesterday and there's fishing shanties in the middle of the lake."

I finished lacing up and handed her the camera. Then we heard what sounded like a fairytale giant pounding his fist with all his might under the suffocating ice, roaring with an angry deep-throated voice for someone to let him out.

"God," she said. "What is that sound?"

"Just the ice setting up, getting stronger. It was 5 degrees last night. C'mon. You can stay by the shore and be the official Olympic photographer."

I pushed off with short uneasy strides but quickly fell into a rhythm of longer and familiar strokes.

Seconds later I was flying through the bright windless morning, weightless, leaning out over my knees, stronger and stronger, blades sharp as diamonds etching into the hard glassy surface. Below me, the ice was so clear I could see the bottom in a way I never had before. It was like looking at the sea through the keel window of a glass bottomed boat. A school of fingerling perch zoomed past me, tiny dolphins keeping me company as I picked up speed.

As I pointed my freezing nose towards Dodge Point, hands clasped behind my back like a long distance speeder skater, a deafening boom echoed below me. It was ten times louder than the one we'd heard along the shore. I changed my mind about skating across the bay and curled towards the shallows. When I got back to our place, Sal was up in the yard, far from the ice, shaking her head.

"I don't trust it whatever you say."

We skied, we snowshoed, we took lots of pictures, and we both decided our final event would be lunch at The Noka Café in Topinabee. When our waitress delivered our favorite meal, patty melts smothered with fried onions, a couple of snowmobilers pulled up in front of the restaurant.

"Did you hear a machine went through the ice on Saturday?" the woman asked as she handed me a tall glass of ice cold milk.

"No we didn't." I said.

"Only four foot deep so nobody drowned. Just wet and real cold. A guy lost his snowmobile. It was a brand new one, too."

A January Thaw
Friday, January 22nd, 2010

Through my office window the retreat of daylight across Mullett Lake was a ballet of pink and white and grey. A hundred yards out, jagged edges of cracked ice zigzagged in a broad ribbon towards the opposite shore. A blue haze dropped from the sky as the sun set.

A seagull settled on neighbor John's boat hoist and stared at a tiny pool of open water where John's well pours into the lake. In a splintered moment of descending dark the bird dove beak first into the shallows and pulled out a crawfish, dancing high into night air with a meal clenched in its teeth. I saw the flash of victory against all odds in his yellow eyes.

Down the shore our neighborhood bald eagle floated into view. He gazed up at the seagull with anger and respect and circled the lake one more time before declaring it closed for the season. Maybe another thaw would come but I could tell he wasn't counting on it.

At this time of year in northern Michigan, mid thirties with sunshine is a heat wave. Patches of green brown grasses poked fun at the beleaguered snow cover.

My cell phone bleated a text message. Our best friends from Ohio were making record time.

I looked around my office. Papers lay all over the place. Manila folders flopped open across the hardwood. Mail screamed 'open me'. A desert house plant yelled something about being thirsty. A cluster of long thick icicles on the corner of the back cabin fell with a thud into piles of silver snow along the outside wall. A sleepy fog rolled out the cedars by the trail and into our yard.

I rose from my studio chair with a push from my forearms and started putting things right in my sacred little workspace. I even watered the needy Mexican palm.

As I waited for my best pal and his family to arrive for a downhill skiing weekend, I organized. And organized. But all I really did was move stacks from one table to another and think about what I needed to do to when the weekend was over.

Dusk had some staying power a month into winter. Between our main cabin and the snow covered rocks along the shore three black squirrels darted up the ash tree hanging over the ice where our dock juts out in summertime.

What are these little guys doing running around like kids at a playground in the middle of January?

Ten minutes later the evening was black as tar. I flipped the switch near the front door and the outside lights sent beams of gold light through the yard.

I found myself praying for colder weather. And deeper snow. I figured I'd regret it but I couldn't help myself. I thought about the merchants counting on brisk snowmobile business. I worried about the ice being thick enough on Moran Bay in St. Ignace come the middle of February. The city hosts the biggest hockey tournament in Michigan with over a hundred teams arriving from all over the country for the U.P. Pond Hockey Championship and they need help from arctic blasts each year. I fretted about our friends skiing in slush over at Nubs Nob.

What about Mackinaw City's Winterfest? The ice carving competition? The outhouse races on the ice? How can you hold a frozen chicken bowling tournament with floppy half frozen poultry?

I joined Sal at the kitchen table.

"They should be here any time."

"This is going be fun. I've really missed them," she replied, not looking up from her book.

"Me, too."

"Are you about to share a new worry with me? I can see it in your face."

 "I was."

 "Don't."

 "Okay."

 "You haven't spent time with Chip since summer."

 "It's been a while. God, it's been almost six months."

 She looked up, taking off her reading glasses.

 "I love it when you guys stay up late and howl like teenagers."

 "We get a little silly by bedtime, don't we?"

 "And tipsy."

 I heard the baritone of a big Chevy engine and looked out the window towards the entrance to our property. A great white suburban with its headlights on high beam curved down our driveway with confidence.

 Our little dog Maizie bounded down the stairs, yelping 'they're here, they're here, they're here!'

Quiet Time
Friday, January 29th, 2010

 For the first time in months, nothing threw itself at us from the grey blue horizon. No duties of stuffing wood into a furnace inside our cottage. No weekend errands or pending adventures. No relatives or friends arriving from South World. The sky stretched far into the next day, lazy in the warm winter's day. Dark and bright one minute to the next. The house rested silent, its ice blanket in piles all around it. I stared at the still uneasy ice out on Mullett Lake through the picture window.

 Winter had stopped to look at itself, surprised at its own mercy. I did the same.

 I wrote a letter to my dad as it began to snow.

Dear Pop:

Things are fine here. Not much going on. Got the generator outlet wired into the garage. I know, down pat, the start up, hook up the cords, and flip the right switches on the panel routine. Reverse order when the power comes back on just like you told me. Not enough power to run anything but the water pump and the house lights. If the power goes out, we'll have water running but not hot water. I can stop worrying about our pipes freezing.

My job is great though I'm still trying to turn it into something bigger. Some uphill sledding to do but that's life. You know that better than anyone. I'm real proud of you for being yourself even though all your health troubles meant you couldn't make to Florida this year to get out of the arctic air in Duluth. At least it's sunny there when it drops below zero. We're usually ten degrees warmer with cloud cover coming at us from all four directions. There's mostly open water and a little pack ice under the Mighty Mac. Fresh snow expected this morning. About three inches. Never thought I'd be so happy to see it. There's something discomforting about last year's grass in the yard in January.

Your grandsons are doing really well.

Max is busy at the studio down in Columbus this month. He's producing albums for a couple of wonderful bands and he's real proud of the music. He's got a girlfriend. He says they eat hotdogs when they go out for food and ramen noodles when they stay in.

Hart's got his hands full in New York. He interns two days a week, works part time, and his school schedule is incredibly demanding. Don't know how he does it. Sometimes we don't hear from him for a couple of weeks.

We miss them terribly.

Sal's pounding away on her next novel. She's on a roll I think. She doesn't let me read it because I always have too much to say and that can ruin her stream of consciousness. She knows me too well.

You and Mom stay warm. We'll try to get over to see you guys when spring arrives. Hang in there.
Love, Don

As I folded the stationery carefully and slid the note into an envelope, I noticed the snow had been falling with conviction for some time. Watching it cover the yard like a down comforter I felt someone standing behind me. When I turned to see who it was, the shadow retreated into the round stones and mortar of the fireplace.

I knew who it was. It was the other me, the one who fears, doubts and worries his way through foul weather and fair. The guy with no health insurance. The man with a backpack of regrets. The soldier of misfortune who likes to slip inside my skin. He'd been reading the letter to my dad over my shoulder.

Outside I retrieved the snow shovel from under the eve of the garage. A rat-tat-tat disturbed the midday air, muffled by thick flakes descending through the trees. Near the top of the tallest dying cedar, a pileated woodpecker, big as a crow, whacked the tree like a machine gun. His crimson head rattled the bark at twenty hits a second. I stood looking up as he made a perfect square hole. His mate joined him on a lower branch, pleased with her boyfriend's work. A small flock of brown grey wrens gathered in a barren poplar to wait for an easy dinner of ants when the giant birds had their fill.

For some reason I placed the shovel over my shoulder and walked to the edge of the shoreline. I stared across the lake as the snow fell fast and soft.

No fishing shanties, no outlines, no snowmobile tracks. No opposite shore, no cracks in the ice. A heaven of colorless pure white.

Sal let our dog Maizie out the side door by the kitchen and she found me wide-eyed by the lake. It was her kind of snow, light as the feather of a dove. In four inches of it, she pretty much disappeared.

I leaned the shovel against the ash tree and crouched down like a baseball catcher, carefully gathering a handful of snow in my gloves. I opened my hand palm up and whispered into it. The weightless powder disappeared.

The Pump Room
Friday, February 12, 2010

Last night our Mullett Lake cottage was a whaling ship riding the murky seas of early spring four hundred miles southeast of Nantucket. Yellow beams creaked above the support columns. Oil lanterns swung gracefully back and forth with the rise and fall of the prow.

In my dream I invited my first mate to my cabin for a dinner of salted mutton, herring and the last of the black potatoes. We carried a full load of whale oil for lamps across New England and most of the states beyond. Mr. Marriott and I shared a triple ration of rum. We told stories until the sun dipped below the horizon. We were confident for the first time in three years. Only four days from home port and our families. Only four days.

I went to bed fully dressed. In the middle of the night I felt someone shaking my shoulder.

"Captain. The sea is up."

"Who is it?"

"Marriott, Sir."

I rolled on my back and stared at the boards above my bunk.

"What is it?"

"The sea is up, Sir."

"The sea is up?"

"It is. We've trimmed the sails. It's a serious storm, Captain."

The cottage roof sank under the weight of midwinter ice and boomed an earthquake through the upstairs bedroom. I sat upright in our bed. Sally breathed deeply, in and out, dreaming her own dreams.

I tiptoed down the hall to the upstairs bathroom, determined not to wake her. How could she sleep through an explosion like that?

When I turned on the faucet, cold water spit in the sink and quit altogether. Hot water the same. A frozen pipe. Damn.

I checked out the rest of the house. No water pressure at all. It wasn't the pipes. It had to be the bloody pump. I pulled on my jeans, threw on my parka, and started for the back cabin through the darkness. It was getting colder by the minute.

Inside the pump room I pulled on the string dangling from the light bulb. When I tried the water in the wash basin, air burped from the spigot. I opened the panel wired for the new portable generator.

This had to be the problem. The day Andy finished the electric work he drove his big truck back into town to get a replacement for a brand new one.

I flipped the breaker for the pump to off and back to on again. I did it twice. I opened the main panel and closed it after trying the same tricks.

My heart sank. The pipes would surely freeze on a night like this. Even if I could reach my plumbing and heating guy in the middle of the night we'd have to lower the lifeboat and abandon ship. It was time to wake Sally and give her the bad news.

As I stepped outside, a vaporous voice echoed down our gravel road.

"Try again."

I stopped and listened.

"What?"

"Don't give up so easily."

I recognized who it was. It was the voice I heard every day as a boy. It was the voice that badgered and chastised me every time I kicked myself about losing a little war.

Back in the pump room, I tried the breakers with the same luck as before.

I flipped down the toilet seat cover and sat down, chin resting in the palms of my hands. The white walls of the small room moved in on me. In the upper corner behind leftover pieces of vinyl siding, I noticed a little wooden box I'd never seen before. Layers of paint had sealed it.

When I pried the thing open with a screwdriver, two fuses looked out at me with the eyes of a child, one orange and the other clear as crystal.

I retrieved a matching pair from our kitchen in the cottage and screwed them into place. As the pump hummed, I heard the voice once more. It drifted through the pump room walls and into the surrounding woods. I couldn't make out the words exactly but I sensed with the hair on the back of my neck that the message was generous. Proud even.

The Mullett Lake Winter Olympinx
Friday, February 19th, 2010

It started when Sal's sister Stephanie arrived in Northern Michigan from Memphis for a long weekend at the cottage.

After more days of melting, a little snow, and more melting, a storm started up about an hour before Sal left to meet the last flight into Pellston. I offered to go with her. I imagined her stranded in a white out.

It was almost 11:00 p.m. when she walked out the door, leaving me with orders to go to bed because I had a meeting real early downtown.

I didn't. As her car disappeared through the snow, I laced up my cross country boots and walked out the kitchen door into blowing clouds of white powder. The boots were warm. I had no intention of skiing. My feet carried me to the drop-off by the lake shore.

I half crawled and half slid down through the rocks and walked out onto the snow covered ice. Thirty yards away, I could barely see the ridge of jagged ice that curved towards Dodge Point. I'd been watching it rise a little bit every day. I'd been telling Sally about how I was worried for the snowmobilers. They might not see it if we got more than four inches. That much was surely on the way.

As I got closer to it, it seemed to disappear. I stepped over it and back again. Not much of a crevice. Not much of a ridge. Just a little hump in the snow. It was time for bed after all.

In the morning I stood blurry-eyed in front of the coffee machine and begged for the dripping to stop. Sally and Steph came down in their flannel patterned pajamas, following the aroma of Columbian beans.

"Hey, Don," Steph said, a holiday tone in her sweet raspy voice. "Fabulous to see you."

We hugged. She smiled. Her short dark hair matted the side of her head.

"What are you girls doing today?"

"We're planning the Mullett Lake Olympinx," said Steph.

"Olympinx?"

"Don't you remember? Six years ago. The summer games in Athens up. You fixed up an old TV in the guest room upstairs and twisted the antenna until I could watch track and field? You know I've always had a thing for the Games."

"Sure. It was a great summer. It was real warm. Can't believe it's been six years."

"Opening ceremony in Vancouver is tonight… and so is ours. Be ready!"

I made sales calls with my partner the whole day and arrived back at Mullett Lake late for dinner.

Sal's brother Dave and his two boys had made it up from Columbus safely. They planned on a day of snowboarding in Harbor Springs and one pegged for the big water park at Boyne Mountain. And of course the Games, plural.

As I threw my coat over the back of a chair, I saw Olympic rings made of felt on the dining table, a neat stack of matching gold, silver and bronze medals as well. Steph, the artist, had been busy.

Sal and Steph went down the list of Olympinx events scheduled for the weekend.

Ice bowling on the lake. A frozen Tyson Cornish game hen for a ball. Little plastic bowling pins purchased in the toy section at Wal-mart ready to go.

Cards. Details to be announced.

Crazy dancing. With music selected by the contestants.

Dishwashing. Judging based on style, speed and effectiveness.

Spoon-on the-nose gymnastics.

And other events to be announced as Steph came up with them.

The boys laughed until their stomachs hurt. They couldn't stop smiling at the thought of the adults in their constellation committed to pure silliness for the next two days. They'd forgotten the controller for their X-box and didn't care.

Sal had her two siblings at her side for the first time in what seemed a thousand years. Every few minutes they giggled. When they plopped down on the couch, they sat close together like toddlers getting their picture taken.

I stuck a big maple log in the woodburner and lit a pile of birch in the big fireplace. John, my plumbing and heating guy, told me that once you have a wood stove, the big hearth blaze sucks all the precious heat up the chimney. I didn't care. It was like lighting the Olympinx flame. I felt like I'd been running with the torch for most of the winter waiting for this.

The Life and Times of a Rookie Referee
Friday, February 26th, 2010

Last weekend I refereed nine games in two days up in St. Ignace at the U.P. Pond Hockey Championship. Over 136 teams from all over the country played on 24 rinks of brilliant shining ice out on Moran Bay.

When I left on Friday late morning the sun was bright and high in the sky. The back seat of the Jeep was stuffed with my parka, my

Sorel boots, a thermos of hot coffee with cream and sugar, and everything else I figured I might need. My first game was scheduled for 1 p.m.

Bearing down on Mackinaw City on I-75, the south and north towers of the Bridge appeared in the distance, immense grey-brown monuments against a perfect blue canvass.

I pulled into the parking lot of the Driftwood Inn and found Scott in the main tent out on the ice. He smiled when he saw me. He was big blonde guy. Muscles all over the place. Sweet smile. He gave me the 21-and-Over Elite Division.

"Thanks for coming. Rink Number One, Donnie."

The first two teams sat on straw bales and laced up their skates. One group from western Canada and the other local boys. When they were ready, I gathered everyone at center ice.

"You guys know the rules. No checking. If you get a penalty for it, it's a goal for the other team. No lifting the puck over the knee."

"Let's go," said a stocky kid from British Columbia. His black greasy hair stuck out in all directions from under his helmet. "We know the rules."

Two games went by without a hitch. But as the second half of the third game got underway, two things happened. Play got rough and the sun softened the two foot high snow banks fashioned as boards. I started calling penalties and arguments broke out.

Every time the puck flew over the melting border of the rink there were more arguments. Every time the puck slid deep into the snow bank there was contention about who touched it last. In pond hockey the referee stands on the sidelines between the two benches and doesn't skate. Sometimes you're a long way from the action.

Luckily, one team won handily. But I'd lost control of the game and knew it. If it'd been a close game there would have been trouble. I drove back to our Mullett Lake cottage thinking about it all the way.

At the dinner table, Sally snapped me out of it with three little words.

"It's your rink."

"I know."

"The players have to know it, too."

Two hours later I lay in bed and gave myself a good talking to before my sore legs led me into a deep mid winter sleep.

Driving down the hill into St. Ignace on Saturday morning I felt ready to be a real referee. I couldn't let another game get away from me. I had five games to do with just a break for lunch. I parked the Jeep in the Shepler parking lot and slowly sipped my coffee. I was early. I wanted to be.

I tracked down Scott and found him looking out from the gate towards a fast rising sun even brighter than the day before. He wore pads and skates and leaned on his stick. He and his old high school buddies had a team in the tournament.

"Hey, Don."

"Hey, Scott."

"You've got Rink Number One again."

"Good."

"You have any trouble yesterday?"

"Nope."

"You've got the 50-and-over guys today."

"I do?" I wasn't sure if I was relieved or disappointed to get the guys my age.

"Yup. First game in 20 minutes."

The day passed with ease. I got to know most of the players like we were teammates. They were in it for fun and fresh air.

I changed the possession rule. Whoever was closest to the puck when it went out of play got to start play again. It made for a smooth flow to the games. They teased me and I teased them right back. We all felt like kids and that seemed to be point of it all by the time the day was over.

The Crow Moon
Friday, March 5th, 2010

The other night I woke up at 4 a.m. and lay in my bed. My eyelids felt like stones, but I couldn't go back to sleep. I didn't know why, I just couldn't. Instead of fighting it I sat up and stuffed my dry feet into my slippers and tiptoed down the stairs to stoke the fire in the woodburner.

I sat down at the dining table and breathed deeply. I took a swallow from the glass of milk I planned on nursing before returning to restlessness upstairs. A pile of maple kindling began to glow, throwing orange and yellows rays between my legs. The wood hissed like an angry cat.

Out the picture window snow sparkled in the moonlight out on Mullett Lake. It seemed a magical version of day, not night. A white fairy tale world filled with crystals and blue shadows. As the fire warmed the room, I felt the muscles in my neck release their burden. My arms fell heavy into my lap. I began to feel sleepy. But I fought it off. This night had invited me to play. How could I refuse?

I opened the side door of the stove and placed two big logs inside. I warmed my hands for a few seconds. A peaty smell filled the room.

I soon found myself standing at the window, wide awake and hypnotized at the same time. A perfect reflection of the fire jumped up and down in the glass. The moon was brighter, higher in the sky than before, putting on a show just for me. I stood there barely blinking for an hour.

Back at the table, I pulled a wool blanket over my knees to enjoy the night's company for a few more minutes. My head drooped. I slumped in the chair. I nodded off. But just for a few seconds. As I pulled my eyes open and reached for the last sip of milk, I sensed someone looking at me. I glanced right, out the window, and spilled milk all over the place.

Eight whitetails stood inches from the window, mesmerized by the glowing fire. Their ears stood up straight. They strained to hear sounds that did not exist. I could see them perfectly in the moon's spotlight. I stood and walked to the window but they didn't flinch. They stood more erect, all eyes searching for the meaning of the mysterious flickering light behind me. I was invisible. A fawn moved away and scratched at the shallow snow around our stone deck.

By the time I slid into the kitchen and returned with a cotton towel to clean up the mess, the little herd had casually moved on. This March was April to them and the older does seemed almost giddy about it.

This was the ritual of The Crow Moon I'd read about. Critters begin to move. Deer seek out patches of grass laid bare by a few days of sun in the low 30's. Families of crows look for easy meals where wild animals make mistakes. The first breath. The awakening.

"What are you doing down there, Don?" asked Sally, awakened by the sound of the crash of my glass. "What's going on?

"I'm watching deer in our front yard."

"Really?"

"Yeah. Look out the guest bedroom windows. They're all over the yard."

She came half way down the staircase.

"C'mon up to bed. You have a big day tomorrow. I've been worrying about you and I need sleep, too."

"Did you see them?"

"Yes. They're beautiful. They're peaceful."

"I'll be right up."

When I finished mopping the floor and the table top, I returned to my chair and pulled it close to the fire. I figured fate had dragged me from my warm and cozy bed and plopped me down to witness the whitetails out my window. Fate had brought me to Cheboygan and was trying to show me why.

A Day Like This a Year Ago
Friday, March 12th, 2010

It was mid morning and the skies were cobalt blue. Out my office window two mallards flew along the shore of Mullett Lake, cupped their wings, did that upside down thing they do to put on the brakes, and splashed feet first into our little inlet bordered by snowless ice. Just enough open water to bring them in. The sun was bright and warm like spring and our yard was mostly bare, way ahead of schedule.

It was a day like this a year ago when we first arrived, our cars stuffed with everything we could jam into them. It was the first of ten trips back and forth to Ohio to keep the moving costs down. Sally and I know our first winter in Northern Michigan could have been a lot worse. Our built-for-summer-only cottage went up in 1936. The craftsmen who framed it out and set the great pine beams in place had no thoughts about a crazy couple deciding to live in it year round.

God, it's been a whole year.

I decided to make one of my lists. Good Fortunes Up North. I typed away as my mind wandered back and forth through the last twelve months.

One. Fred at Village Auto scoured the internet for a week to find a part and save me $200.

Two. John, Dave, and Andy took our winter plumbing, heating and electrical challenges to heart like we were relatives from Texas without a clue about what it's like at twenty degrees below. They knew I needed serious help the minute they met me.

Three. Gary and Janis and Mary and Nancy and Dan and everyone else at the Tribune drew me into the newspaper world. That was the moment the sails of my family ship caught some wind after sitting in a dead calm for too long.

Four. The McGregors down at the Mullett Lake Country Store got their liquor license. That was big for all of us. I get out-of-date tonic for free from old Bob. I'm not supposed to tell anyone.

Five. Jim arrived in his red pickup with the big plow whenever I started lacing up my boots to give the giant Toro another try after a big snow. Turns out I didn't need the snowblower much after all. It's a good thing. Every time I used the machine the tendon in my right elbow felt like a rubber band about to snap.

I added story after comment after story until my fingertips hurt. My back got stiff and sore. I stood up, walked around, and opened the storm door window. The year's first warm wind caressed my cheeks. I could taste the temperature. It was almost 60 degrees. Free of ice at last, our little well creek splashed like the big streams. I stood there for five minutes with my eyes closed.

Back at my desk I started writing again and then stopped. Out the window towards the lake I saw our bald eagle had returned. He soared high in the sky over the dark grey ice. With every circle he descended several feet and drew closer to shore.

That's when I realized the title of my list was all wrong. These things were not made of fine luck or good fortune. Not coincidence or happenstance. The whims of fate had nothing to do with it.

I erased the title with a swipe of the cursor. I typed in a new title.
People Up North

This was better. No matter what the tougher side of luck might deliver in tomorrow's mail, Sal and I were pretty darn smart to make Cheboygan our home last year.

Looking for Lizzie
Friday, March 19th, 2010

Last night at 10 pm I noticed our dog Maizie's spotted pink skin showing through her short haired coat as she lay on her side. She panted as though I had her under a hair dryer. The place she owned in front of the woodburner on the Chinese carpet was her comfort zone.

She rose from the floor, stretched with straight forelegs, and pulled herself backwards like a little yoga trainer. Her tongue hung to the floor. Her ears popped up. The helpless beggar look. It never failed. She got the doggie snack tucked into my pants pocket.

I couldn't help thinking about what I learned about dogs back in college. They're all descended from a group of Mongolian wolves. They crept closer and closer to man and his fire for warmth and scraps. They acted like puppies for the privilege, eventually joining our hunts and sleep. Sally has grown tired of my anthropology lessons over the years, claiming I use facts like medieval weapons over and over again.

She started up the stairs with a thick book in one hand and reading glasses in the other, successfully dodging yet another of my insights about the cultural interdependence of man and canine.

"Is it time for bed already?" I asked.

"It is for me."

"Okay. We'll be right behind you."

Sally suffered greatly for loving Maizie like a youngest child. She was allergic to dogs and she let Maizie curl under the comforter on our bed each night.

"See if Maizie will go outside with you first."

Maizie refused to follow me out the door whenever Sal retired first. Last night, for some reason, I was sure she'd go with me.

She tore through the brown grass lit by our outside lights and into the darkness beyond. She disappeared completely for ten minutes but I wasn't worried. I knew she was looking for Lizzie.

Lizzie was a big, happy yellow Labrador. She spent her summers two yards south along the shore. She lost her battle with longevity last November. Neighbors Barb and Kate and Robb, Lizzie's people, were still heartbroken. Suddenly I missed Lizzie more than I could talk about. The beautiful early spring weather had opened the wound. They'd be up in a couple of months without her.

Late in life the old girl learned to overcome her fear of slippery surfaces in my kitchen. I'd tease her with one of Maizie's dog treats to coax her across the smooth blue linoleum. Her eyes were wet golden almonds. Maizie hated the attention I gave her but they were close friends. Maizie used her like a giant easy chair whenever she felt like it. And that was a lot. I didn't cry when I heard the news that Lizzie had died. I guess I was too worried about our friends.

Now it was mine and Maizie's turn to mourn.

The black night seemed endless. A single star escaped cover and followed along above me. I walked with a heavy heart through neighbor John's place to Lizzie's domain. It was a perfectly still night with no wind and no moon. The silhouette of Lizzie's house appeared through tall shadowy maples. I drew a great breath through my nose and into my lungs. Maizie snuck up on me and nudged my ankle with her nose, slopping her affectionate wetness all over the laces of my shoe.

"You couldn't find her, could you?" I asked.

Before the Lightning Strikes
Friday, March 26th, 2010

The sight of water moving again amid the plain of thin blue ice on the north end of Mullett Lake made me drunk with hope. The mid afternoon sun was high and warm. Dark blue rivers, streams and creeks weaved through the shimmering glass.

The stubborn north breeze blowing over Dodge Point shifted effortlessly to the south. Grey clouds moved in. A flock of a hundred plus gulls flocked into view from the Huron horizon. Two Christmas trees out on the lake marked abandoned fishing holes.

Thirty or so American Mergansers whistled past me as I stood along the beach. They landed hard like anxious pilots on the deck of an aircraft carrier. My eagle friend was a spot of black in the sky where two wispy clouds held hands. The first moments of astronomical spring reached out to touch the earth.

Two gulls peeled off from the rest and coasted into our cove. I didn't move a muscle. Round and round they flapped and screeched as though they'd been waiting for our clear waters for a thousand years. They were returning. They'd been surviving along the rocks and over the sandy colored water of the west shore for many more eons than Sally and I.

I made like a statue. The two birds didn't recognize me as human. They settled into our pond made by the ice. One of them stared into the clear shallow pool while the other looked me in the eye. If I hadn't breathed so deeply they might not have retreated to their companions out on the cold ice.

All at once the largest sheets began to move, inches at first, and then with conviction. The pines out in the middle rose, teetered and disappeared. Just two weeks ago I watched a little white pickup drive away from the spot, hauling a wood shanty on a sled.

Thousands of small stones filled our normally sandy coast, somehow dragged into our small half moon bay by the odd winter. I could walk out where the seagulls landed with only the soles of my shoes getting wet, like Jesus in sneakers.

The lake was two feet down. Without spring rains, the docks in summer would look like a delta waterfront at low tide. I hadn't realized how far it had fallen. Would I now have to pray for rain when the yellow rays of a gentle early season felt so good?

I walked to neighbor John's permanent dock of ancient wood and surveyed the remnants of a strange winter from there. His side of the structure, his beautiful low beachfront of soft sand, was filled with hand sized gravel.

Back on my property, I sat on the shelf of round stones my best friend from Duluth helped me build as a retention wall against hard waves from the east. I remembered the taste of the cold beer I drank as we made the barrier one rock at a time.

I looked up at the sun still bright through the haze. I closed my eyes and squeezed them tight to make darkness. I asked for something from my maker.

Thunderstorms. Bring us April thunderstorms. Dampen the woods filled with dry grasses before the lightning strikes. Don't worry about my leaky roof. I'll get it fixed.

Surveying the Back Forty
Friday, April 2nd, 2010

Some people have a Back Forty they prowl when spring arrives. They walk their woods and fields to see what winter left behind. I toured mine yesterday after a long day on the road selling what I sell.

I pried my borrowed wood pile planks from the mossy ground beneath the cedars and carried them back to the stack next to neighbor John's garage. I'd judged the winter supply of maple for the woodburner almost perfectly, Sally had said, though I didn't deserve the credit. Everyone in northern Michigan knows we had generous temperatures and no killer storms.

Over the septic field beyond our gravel turnaround, I walked west towards the North Central Michigan Trail. The forest floor cracked under my feet. The smell of drying leaves filled my nose. All around me, aspens and old maples swayed in the breeze, breathing in the heat of a dry warm early spring.

I crossed the hard pan of the trailbed and found the ditch bone dry. I found a stump for sitting. The angle of the lumberman's cut made a perfect stool for viewing the sweep of the open southern sky.

I sat there for a half hour shirking the responsibilities. As my small wooded cathedral warmed up, I struggled to move an inch towards the Mullett Lake cottage. My legs were lead. My eyes refused to blink.

Something, I knew not what, lifted my body back on the path home.

Forty steps towards the lake I realized what it was. Dinnertime.

"Lake trout," Sally said as she swung my plate under my nose. What were you doing out there?"

"Just looking around. Gosh, this smells incredible."

"What did you find?"

"The woods are tinder dry. It's no wonder there's an open burning ban."

"What'll you do with all the yard waste you've been collecting?"

"Just wait I guess."

When I finished the last bite of wild rice, I sat down at my computer and Googled "forest fires of northern Michigan." One date kept reaching out from the monitor: October 16, 1908.

There'd been a drought for six months with no more than a sprinkle the entire summer and into the fall. Slash from twenty years of heavy lumbering lay in the new growth forests, ready for a spark, and then it happened. Someone decided the breeze was right for a clearing burn but the winds shifted suddenly and mightily to the southwest. Fires raged from Saginaw to Cheboygan. 200 people on a train filled with families trying to escape the blaze in Metz perished when the great fire surrounded them. Over fifty inland lakes boiled. Hot ash set the Sawdust Mountain in Cheboygan on fire, threatening the entire city. A hundred angry blazes raged throughout the Straits, keen to merge into one enormous furnace. Two days later when all seemed lost, a damp wind blew in from Lake Huron and turned the fires into smoke.

I read no further. Even though the mercury dropped well below freezing by bedtime, I didn't make a fire to warm the cottage for the night like I usually did. I turned up the thermostat. The baseboard heaters clicked and clacked, happy for the surge of electricity bringing them back to life.

Our Planet is Flat
Friday, April 9, 2010

All matter is made of water, fire, air and earth. Our planet is flat. The world is a globe and the sun moves around it. The sound barrier can not be broken. The moon is out of reach.

Scientists have been wrong more than a few times, but Mother Nature never errs. Spring rains had finally come. Temperatures had dropped to the low 40s after weeks of incessant way-above-average days and nights. Wet snow was in the forecast.

I shivered uncontrollably on the North Central Michigan Trail like our dog Maize does when the slightest breeze blows through our open cottage windows. The path was riddled with puddles and my pant cuffs were soaked. The wind poured off the grey water. Black and purple clouds raced across the sky from their hiding place to the east. They'd been waiting for a chance to visit Cheboygan for a month.

Inside the Mullett Lake store, Bob the Elder stuffed the things I usually bought into a bag before I told him what I wanted.

"Back to Northern Michigan weather I guess," he said.

He looked dog tired. More than usual. He'd let his beard grow since Labor Day. The register popped open as he took a twenty from my cold red fingers.

"I know."

"We need the rain but it still makes things a little gloomy around here."

"Sure does."

"You walk down here, Don?"

"Yup. Doctors orders."

"Doctor?"

"Not really. Walking was Sally's idea."

An hour later, I was on my way to Harbor Springs for business through a soup of relentless drizzle. I nearly plowed into a rafter of turkeys in the middle of the road a mile past Pellston. The blurry hills made me want to turn around but I didn't. My nose was just a few inches from the windshield. I smelled overheated rubber through the defroster vent.

When I finished my last meeting, the first thunder rolls of spring pushed me into my old Jeep and then a storm let loose. Half way home, a low lying spot along Richardson Road was a great swampy lake between two farms. I heard the white crack of lightning and drove through the water slowly, not knowing if I should use more speed or keep it to a crawl.

Headlights awash in sideways rain came at me one after another. I caught a glimpse of an unshaven man in suspenders behind the wheel of his heavy duty pickup truck, crawling past me in the on-coming lane. Like me, he looked worried about the sudden darkness. I couldn't see a thing along Church Road so I pulled over. The radio played an old country song by George Jones. For the last twenty miles I hadn't been aware of the music at all, only the invisible road and my wipers. When the rain let up I started for home again.

The sky lifted as I turned off the Straits Highway towards our place. I stopped where I always do to look at the lights of the cottage through the cedars and beech trees. On the path to the front door, my feet felt heavy. Patches of faded blue sky opened above me.

"How was your day?" Sally asked as she walked down the stairs.

"The ride home was miserable."

"Why?"

"The first big one."

"Big what?"

"Thunderstorm."

"Isn't that what you were hoping for?"

"Yes it was."

In the shower a few minutes later I stood under the hot water for longer than I should have. I thought about the turkeys and how I could have killed them all if I'd been thinking about anything but driving. I imagined myself behind the wheel of an amphibious auto-mobile from the 1950s. I saw flashes of lightning when I closed my eyes.

Our First Garden Ever
Friday, April 16th, 2010

Sally was heading down south for the weekend, leaving our Mullett Lake cottage and my incessant ramblings for a few days.

"Would you take this bag to the car for me? Don't let Maizie out."

"Sure."

Maizie peered out the window as I followed Sally to the drive-way. Our little dog was a sad mascot, her head tilted in disappoint-ment. She wasn't going along on Sal's trip.

The morning was filled with gold light and a shock blue sky. The grass in the yard was really green for the first time. As Sal pulled out of the driveway, she opened the window of her newly washed red Camry and yelled a last second instruction.

"Don't make any major decisions on the garden while I'm gone. Please."

"I won't. Only grunt work, I promise."

She didn't hear me.

I watched her car turn the far corner past the hedges lining North Silver Beach Road. I opened our barely operable garage door. Inside were tools forgotten since the last days of autumn. I pulled the tools I figured I needed from a stack in the corner.

My tape measure in hand, I calculated the dimensions Sally had prescribed for our first garden ever. I drove pine stakes at the imagi-nary corners. The spade with the broken tip slipped into the soft black earth. It cut through the sod like it was made of tar.

The spot Sally had picked was wet and dense under the surface. After twenty minutes, each shovel of six inch turf weighed in at hundred pounds as far as my back was concerned.

Row after row I levered one chunk of sod after another into the pit I was creating. I began to sweat. I got on my knees and whacked the dirt from every piece I heaved. An hour later I could hardly feel my legs. My shoulders ached. The bottom of my feet felt like I'd been tortured.

Like a man painting himself into the center of a room, I'd dug around the edges of the plot toward the middle. I'd made a perfect resting place under the rising sun. I jammed the shovel into the old flower beds lining the south side of the back cabin.

Lying on the dewy grass I looked up at white contrails writing words from one horizon to the other. As I began to drift off, a smell from somewhere deep in my past asked me to remember something. I folded my arms behind my head. I shivered as dampness soaked through my shirt.

I closed my eyes against the bright light. I saw my mom behind the wheel of our cream 1961 Dodge station wagon, driving along a two lane blacktop summer highway in northern Minnesota. We'd just left our log cabin on Grand Lake. Her dark hair was tucked behind her ears. She was smiling and it was hot. The windows were all cranked down. My pig-tailed little sister sat in the front and leaned on the door, making an airplane of her hand out the window. My older brother and sister and I held our noses in the back seat as we passed farm after farm after a heavy overnight storm. We all wore cowboy shirts and cowboy boots. Four kids in four years. I'm pretty sure Mom was dropping us off at my Uncle Sandy's place on Sunset Lake ten miles away. We were happy. Mom even more.

The smell of life hidden under the thick lawn, uncovered by my work, had triggered a Technicolor memory. Of that I was sure. A fresh wind from the lake touched my forehead. Miraculously, with no help whatsoever from the Advil in my jeans pocket, the pain wracking my joints and muscles disappeared.

The Silhouette of a Loon
Friday, April 23rd, 2010

After a long day on the road last Monday, I changed into my sweatpants and sweatshirt and barefooted to the end of our newly-re-installed dock, the first one on Mullett Lake from Dodge Point to Long Point.

I'd been imagining the feel of the wood planks on the soles of my feet during the long ride back from the Upper Peninsula. The day before had been summer-like, but now it was barely 50 degrees and the lake was churning. From the dock I could just make out the silhouette of a loon bobbing through he waves, his head held high as though he was looking for the mate he hadn't seen since fall.

Four giant gulls soared closer to me, screeching like they were mad at each other. One of them spied an evening meal swimming close to the surface and dove into the lake and then rose clumsily into the air with a minnow in its throat.

The dock shook and rattled as I jumped up and down to stay warm. I started shivering uncontrollably. After twenty minutes, a whiff of smoke from our woodburner tracked me down and told me to return to the cottage. But for some reason I could not.

Instead I sat down and stuck my feet in the water. I knew it was dumb but I had to do it. I forced myself to endure the cold. A break in the clouds rewarded me. The sun threw a warm blanket across my back. The water turned sky blue before my eyes.

The euphoria didn't last long. When I felt cold flowing from the frigid water to my head, I stood up and wobbled down the dock back to shore. It was hard to walk totally numb from the knees down.

"Dinner in a minute," Sally said as I sat down by the wood stove. "Your feet are purple. What the heck were you doing out there?"

"Absolutely nothing."

"Okay."

I pulled a chair closer to the fire.

"Actually I put my feet in the lake until I couldn't stand it any more."

"You hate the cold."

"That's true."

"Was it some kind of test or something?"

"Maybe it was."

"Did you pass the test?"

"I think so. I haven't dared myself to do something in a long time."

After dinner, with the first novel I'd read in ages tucked under my arm, I drew hot water in the tub and climbed in. I read two chapters and kept the hot water running. I thought about the loon alone out on the lake, swimming and diving and waiting for its partner to arrive. I wondered if the bird had flown south the first time on a dare or a promise.

Abandoned Cottages
Friday, April 30th, 2010

Last Sunday we drove the Jeep to Topinabee for breakfast at the Noka Café. It'd been a month since Sally and I made the pilgrimage. The idea of two perfect over-easy eggs and corned beef hash had hit us simultaneously. Besides, an easterly storm had come up in the night. For hours it shook our cottage on Mullett Lake until it screamed for mercy. White caps hurdled our dock like my little pier wasn't there. By mid-morning, with the storm gaining strength, we needed a break.

For the most part we ate in silence and read our favorite sections of the newspaper. I said something about how dry the forests were. She looked at me like she didn't need to hear it again.

Back home I realized why the wind was racing through the cottage. We'd taken the storm windows out, the ones facing the lake, and replaced them with our old rusty screens.

Sally retreated upstairs to work on her book.

"Hey Sal," I yelled from the bottom step. "I'm going on a few errands. Got a few things to get in town."

"Great. Pick up burgers and buns and we'll grill tonight." I could tell she was already at her computer. The likelihood of a barbecue in a northeaster wasn't very good. I kept my trap shut with all my might.

I had a few things to buy and fetch and now I had a few more. But what I really possessed was an afternoon to go wherever I wanted. Sally needed some space. I'd heard it in her voice for more than a week.

As I got behind the wheel of the Jeep, I told it to ramble where it pleased. At the Straits Highway it turned north towards Cheboygan. The wind assaulted us as we crawled through downtown at barely the speed limit. Crossing the Mackinac Bridge, I realized it was me doing the driving not the old Jeep. Something was pulling me to the Upper Peninsula.

The sun forced its way through racing clouds. I slowed to the speed limit. To both sides of the great expanse, blue fought grey in the choppy waters. In the distance, a single ferry fought its way through the Straits towards Mackinac Island.

After paying the toll and curling west on US Highway 2, it donned on me where I was going. I was returning to the empty cottages at the mouth of the Pointe Aux Chene River on Lake Michigan. Back in September I'd spent two hours poking around the place. I'd taken a few photographs and printed them and tacked them to the pine board walls around my computer monitor. The abandoned little cabins, with their peeling paint, had looked down on my keyboard all winter long.

I parked in the gravel roundabout in front of the first building.

Everything was the same except the lookout stand. It had suffered a fire. The posts were charcoal but still holding.

I locked the Jeep and started for the reeds below the bridge. Two jet black cormorants, as big as eagles, flopped into their perch on the old oak hanging over the marsh. They ignored me and I them. The path led where it did before, to a beach full of perfectly round stones. I sat on a boulder as big as a truck and watched clouds skimming the horizon at the speed of light. A great ore boat, unfazed by the high winds, crossed my line of sight as it headed out into the endless waters of Lake Michigan.

After twenty minutes, I walked back to the cabins that fascinated me so much last fall. I walked down the road past them all to the last one. I pushed at the rotting door and it fell backwards with me on top of it. Inside I noticed dirty clothes strewn over a musty thin mattress on the wood floor. I felt like an intruder and left.

Driving home I wondered about what had pulled me back to Point Aux Chene. Suddenly I knew what it was. I'd needed to come back to the place I'd felt fear and loneliness, to those little cabins that seemed to feel the same way. Things were different for me now and I had wanted to make sure of it.

First Swim of the Season
Saturday, May 8th, 2010

Last Saturday was summer hot. Even so, I'm pretty sure I took the season's first swim in Mullett Lake. Not that it was much of a dip; it lasted maybe 1.5 seconds. Nobody goes for a swim on the second day of May in Northern Michigan.

When I walked around the cottage to the front yard, I saw Sally sitting in the wooden chaise with the green cushions. The sun stroked her hair with shards of gold. The lawn grew an inch while I stood there.

I sat in the straight back chair next to her, our only real beach towel wrapped around my waist. It's an orange one with a quilted pattern of flowers faded into cotton. I pulled on a t-shirt and jammed my feet into my leather sandals.

"What're you doing?" I asked.

"Reading my book."

"What are you reading?"

"My book."

"Sorry."

Her grey blue eyes returned to a world populated by people other than me.

As I stood up, Sal suddenly laid her book on the grass. She motioned me to follow her to the two bicycles stashed under the stairs of the back cabin.

"This weather won't last. Let's go."

I nodded and followed her out the driveway towards the North Central Michigan Trail. My wet bathing suit squeaked on the seat.

"How far are we going?" I yelped from ten yards in the rear.

"I don't know. Until you get too tired, I suppose."

Turning south towards Topinabee I stood up on the pedals and pumped my way past Sally like a boy out of school early, pedaling home to meet his pals. Left, right, up, down, faster and faster. I left Sally a hundred yards behind me as I cruised under a canopy of budding aspens along the old railway line. My tires hummed louder as I picked up speed.

A blue jay screamed at me to slow down but I would have none of it. On either side of me, fallen cedars and stumps and green tipped bushes were just a blur. Sitting back on the seat, I flipped my sunglasses down and pumped even harder. This trip down the lake shore seemed much easier than ever. There was no way Sal could keep up with me at this pace.

I stopped where we always stop, over the trestle bridge at Mullett Creek, three miles from our cottage. Sal rolled up beside me as I got off the bike.

"Aren't you Mr. Speedy."

"That was great. I haven't really gone for it on two wheels for ages."

"Ready to head back?"

"Sure."

She started out slowly, steady, and then picked up the pace. I caught up with her with no trouble. Then my legs turned to lead pipes. My heart pressed against my ribs. She pulled away with ease. It was the first time I realized there was a slight uphill slope going home. I broke out in a sweat from head to toe, gave up, and started walking beside the bike. My wet bathing trunks chaffed my inner thighs.

I arrived home eons after Sal. She'd started the charcoal and was working in the garden. Maizie, our little terrier, ran up to me in sympathy but suddenly changed her mind. She looked at me instead with disappointment. She raised her ears and cocked her head. She was asking me to explain myself.

"Okay. I know. I'll do better next time."

An Old Familiar Voice
Saturday, May 15th, 2010

Early last Thursday morning before work I stared out at Mullett Lake from my office window. An orange-red buoy bobbed wildly in the unforgiving wind above the great sandbar two miles out.

The coffee burned my tongue but I hardly noticed. All night long I'd rolled my blankets into twine as I tossed and turned. I was as exhausted as I'd ever been in my life.

The sky had been in a hurry over Northern Michigan for days. Dark grey arrived and retreated, making way for blinding bursts of unexpected sunlight. The eastern storm didn't care.

A friend recently told me that people in Montana built special rooms in their basements to deafen Big Sky country that can last for weeks.

I wanted one of those rooms.

Sal came down the stairs for coffee.

"Morning," she said as she cleared her throat. "You sleep well?"

"No."

"What was it this time?"

"The vent above the bathroom screeched like a wounded rabbit all night."

"I know," she piped. "This wind won't last forever."

Sal rolled her eyes and turned for the kitchen. Maizie, our little terrier, stayed behind and gave me that huffy look for a few seconds before racing through the living room.

Alone again I just couldn't keep from staring at the waves. As they rolled under the dock, plumes of green and white spray splashed the wood planks. Big frothy whitecaps put on a show of strength, each trying to better the one before.

Then an old familiar voice whispered over my shoulder.

"Get it together. This heavy wind is fixing things around here."

It was Mr. Conscience stopping by for talk.

"You're right. We had a good soaker yesterday afternoon."

"That's right."

"Can I pray for the wind to stop?"

"No. God has other matters to deal with. I would say bigger stuff than today's weather report from Cheboygan."

Ten minutes later I was dressed in my jacket and tie and ready to run back and forth across the Mighty Mac. I gulped down another cup of coffee, and poured one more for the road.

Inside the Jeep I watched the pines and budding poplars fly by along I-75 as I reached the outskirts of Mackinaw City. I looked up at the blue and red and yellow tubes of the water park and then gazed out at the towers of the bridge through the mist. I could barely make out the silhouette of Mackinac Island. I made two sales calls in St. Ignace and two in Cedarville and one back in Cheboygan and met some wonderful hard working people.

As the Jeep wandered down Church Road on the way home, Mr. Conscience appeared out of nowhere in the passenger seat. I ignored him. He smiled and screwed off the top of a Pepsi bottle. He turned on the heater and rubbed his hands together. He rolled his window down and let the haze moisten his brow. He put his hand on his forehead and ran his hand through his long silver hair. I imagined him fading away with a smile on his face, and then he was gone.

Two Ravens in Our Yard
Saturday, May 29th, 2010

Last Sunday morning I sat in my chair and felt no creative energy at all. It was a quiet and warm morning. Every smell coming through the screens said summer had taken over.

My home office was cluttered like an absent minded professor's. I had a hundred notes tacked to the knotted pine walls. Books I'd been meaning to read lay about the oak floor like rejected pets. The week before I'd finished a year of columns for the Daily Tribune. I was working like a maniac at my new job. Now, all of a sudden, my fingers refused my orders. The keyboard was lonely but I didn't care.

Two ravens, as big as vultures, landed in the long green grass between John's yard and mine. They'd hung around our shore at Mullett Lake for a month earlier in the spring but a few weeks ago I saw four or five wrens hassle them to kingdom come and figured they'd never come back after that whipping. But the tuxedoed pair had other ideas.

They looked back and forth, scoping things out, like burglars in a back alley. They angled along the creek bed into emerald shadows by the spruce trees.

The first sentries to sound the alarm were the robins. Then the finches and sparrows chimed in. I watched an air force of protective mothers drive the black intruders over the hills beyond the Straits Highway.

Out on the lake, speedboats and pontoons made their first wakes in the glassy water. A soft blue sky emerged from the haze. Two Canada geese led their pint sized brood past the end of our dock.

I rose from my seat and stepped out the front door. A patch of fog the size of a football field floated over the middle of the lake. I'd seen it before, in late June last year. The placid waters had warmed rapidly during the night. The vapor, unable to rise against cooler air dropping from above, had no where to go.

Dodge Point basked in the rising northern sun. A single seagull flapped past me, eyeing the shallows in front of our place. I recognized his bent wingtip and the brown spots on his back. He'd been in our little cove when the ice first disappeared. He was back. Unlike the mergansers that made a home along the rocks, he hated zebra muscles. He liked gourmet food: crawfish. He looked at me in the eye as he had in March. He told me again that this was his domain, not mine.

A faint breeze wiped my brow, not strong enough to stir the water but fit enough to make me realize I was empty headed. I wasn't ready for writing or anything else on my God forsaken list. I'd made one every Friday since Sal and I moved to Northern Michigan and it occurred to me as I retrieved more coffee that I should stop making lists for a while.

Sally found me sitting on the sand by the shore.

"You want some company?"

"Yes."

She scrambled down the stone path and plopped down beside me.

"It's really summer," she said, taking a swig from her insulated coffee mug.

"It is."

"What should we do today, work in the garden?"

"No."

"Why not?"

"I don't know. I just haven't the will to do anything."

"Sure you do."

"No. I really don't."

"What gives?"

"I told you. I don't know."

"Then don't do a thing all day."

"What?"

"Read a book from cover to cover."

"I don't think I could."

"Why not?"

"I'd feel guilty the whole time. We have so much to do around here and I've got thousands of words to write before noon tomorrow."

"I'll get you a book right now. One I know you'll like."

She got up and took the slate steps back to the upper yard.

I knew she was right. I had to take some time off and make a vacation out of the misty rays crossing our property. I went back inside, sat at the computer, and turned it off.

My Uncle Sandy
Saturday, June 5th, 2010

Sally was down in Columbus for the Memorial Day weekend to see her dad for the first time in ages. She was having dinner with our son Max, too. The two of them were planning an outing for cheap but good looking clothes to help him find a second job. She expected Max to ask for a run to the grocery for a case of Ramen noodles and other staples. We'd put it in her trip budget.

I had mounds of work to catch up on and exactly one chore while she was gone.

"Water the garden," she had said the night before as we climbed into bed. "It's supposed to be hot."

The next morning as I soaked the vegetable plot along the back cabin, I looked out at Mullett Lake. Waves lapped at the rocks and sand. Robins yelled at each other. I imagined I could hear worms squirming for deeper ground.

Then a memory as real as the breeze on my forehead snuck up behind me and clicked its heels.

It was the mid 1970's. A rare hot July day had settled over Northern Minnesota. I was mixed up as a salad. My father and I had hardly spoken for two months. Things were going badly for him at work and I was too concerned about finding my way in the world to take the time to understand how he felt.

Somehow My Uncle Sandy knew what we were both going through. He's my dad's kid brother. Back then he had his own hell to deal with. My cousins were confused about his divorce and taking sides, things were odd for everyone. Yet, he still took time to comfort me. Dreams were involved, he had said, and dreams were as important as rain.

One time that summer, he toiled between rows of cabbage and lettuce in his great oval garden high above the cabin he built himself when we were little runts. It was perfect therapy for him. His dark green suspenders held up his jeans. He carried weight around his middle like I do now.

He smiled with the hot sun on his brow. He stood up and wiped his forehead with his handkerchief as I helped weed between rows.

"So what are your plans?" he said as he leaned on the handle of an old spade shovel. It was high noon and humid. Sweat rolled off his brow like a waterfall.

"I don't have any, Uncle Sandy. I only know I've got to do something that's only about me."

"I remember the feeling." He pointed at the rows of green and yellow cabbage and lettuce. "This is the best growing season I've ever seen."

"Why?"

"Cool nights with rain. Hot days like today."

"It's too hot if you ask me."

"It's never too hot in a garden if you've got water."

I watched him bend over, pluck a nearly ready cucumber, and pull a salt shaker from his hip pocket. He devoured it ten seconds.

My daydream ended when our terrier Maizie circled me, asking me with her dark brown eyes to chase her around our garage. I obliged and ran out of breath on my second pass around her imaginary racetrack.

The waves on the lake turned grey. I tried to conjure the feeling of that day with Uncle Sandy so many years ago, but as hard as I tried, I couldn't.

A much cooler breeze pranced across the water. I stepped into the wet and black land inside the garden fence. I turned to admire the gate I'd made of chicken wire and old boards two weeks before.

Weeds were hard to find. I dropped on my knees in the corner by the teepee of sticks Sal had built for the cucumbers. I dug into the ground with a three-pronged hook and loosened the dense top soil.

I couldn't see back 40 years, but I could smell my way home well enough.

A Mallard Family Reunion
Sunday, June 20th, 2010

There were five generations of mallards having a picnic on our dock on Mullett Lake last Monday morning. I counted twenty drakes on the pine boards near our Shore Station, happy to be communing with fathers, brothers and cousins and a single hen. The rest of the girls were just off the nest, their little peepers close behind them all over the place in the stirring water.

The east wind was a whisper, warm but getting colder by the minute and dark grey like winter ice. Summer was on holiday.

Sally brought me another cup of coffee while I tied the leather laces of my new shoes.

"What's your day like," she asked.

"Nuts."

"I thought you were going to say that."

"I know. I sound like a broken phonograph."

"You need to take a break."

"I can't afford to. I'm behind on just about everything."

For some reason we both looked out through the picture window at the same time. The greenheads and brown feathered female had gathered company. Five Canada geese were raising their young in the miniature whitecaps. Thirty or so seagulls had joined the party.

"Why do they like our place so darn much?" she asked me.

"I've never seen anything like it."

"Maybe they're trying to tell us something."

"Like what."

"Like raising kids is the whole deal."

"We've done that," I countered.

"You don't stop being a parent once you start."

"We're so far away from our boys."

"It's been good for them."

Sal placed her hand on my shoulder for a second. I barely no ticed when she disappeared upstairs to her office bedroom. A light rain wafted through our bay. I saw Dodge Point to the north retreat in a fog.

I didn't hear her footsteps coming back down the stairs.

"This is where we're supposed to be."

"I know, Sal."

"They've both promised to make it up this summer."

On the way to town in my rusted Jeep, I shivered for a few seconds before powering up all four windows and turning the heater knob to the lowest setting. Up the hill past Polish Line Road, a vivid daydream began. I pulled in the driveway of the shuttered Inverness Elementary School, made a circle under the pines, and pointed the grill of the Cherokee at the Straits Highway. I sipped my coffee and turned off the engine. As a caravan of red pickups blew mist off the asphalt, I closed my eyes and leaped towards a future downstream.

I saw shops downtown filled with customers; Main Street Cheboygan busy like it was a hundred years ago. I saw charter fishing boats lined up on the river in the early morning sun, loading up with families heading out to Lake Huron. I saw launches leaving for daylong trips down the Inland Waterway. I saw a broad canopied dock below a great birch bark building on the plain over the footbridge. Towards the lighthouse, a ferry spouted a golden spray high into the bright blue sky.

From the last row of seats in the Opera House, I witnessed the graduating class of the college receive their diplomas. Like a man with wings, I flew over the new port, out towards the mouth of the river. Two great ships lay in anchor waiting for their turn to load at the Cheboygan docks.

When I opened my eyes, it seemed like years had passed, but strangely, I felt younger. I started the Jeep and began my drive to work through a low drifting fog.

But I wasn't alone. The dream had hitched a ride.